Binxing Fang, Yan Jia (Eds.)
Online Social Network Analysis

Also of interest

Online Social Network Analysis, Volume 2
B. Fang, Y. Jia, 2018
ISBN 978-3-11-059777-6, e-ISBN (PDF) 978-3-11-059941-1,
e-ISBN (EPUB) 978-3-11-059792-9

Online Social Network Analysis, Volume 3
B. Fang, Y. Jia, 2018
ISBN 978-3-11-059784-4, e-ISBN (PDF) 978-3-11-059943-5,
e-ISBN (EPUB) 978-3-11-059793-6

Web Applications with Javascript or Java, Volume 1
G. Wagner, M. Diaconescu, 2018
ISBN 978-3-11-049993-3, e-ISBN (PDF) 978-3-11-049995-7,
e-ISBN (EPUB) 978-3-11-049724-3

Web Applications with Javascript or Java, Volume 2
G. Wagner, M. Diaconescu, 2018
ISBN 978-3-11-050024-0, e-ISBN (PDF) 978-3-11-050032-5,
e-ISBN (EPUB) 978-3-11-049756-4

Trusted Computing
D. Feng, 2017
ISBN 978-3-11-047604-0, e-ISBN (PDF) 978-3-11-047759-7,
e-ISBN (EPUB) 978-3-11-047609-5

Online Social Network Analysis

Volume 1: Structure and Evolution

Edited by
Binxing Fang, Yan Jia

DE GRUYTER

PUBLISHING HOUSE OF ELECTRONICS INDUSTRY
http://www.phei.com.cn

Editors
Prof. Binxing Fang
Chinese Academy of Engineering
Building A, Tri-Tower
No. 66-1 Zhongguancun East Road
100190 Beijing, Haidian District
China

Prof. Yan Jia
National University of Defense Technology
No. 109 Deya Road, Kaifu Strict
410073 Changsha, China

ISBN 978-3-11-075628-9
e-ISBN (PDF) 978-3-11-059937-4
e-ISBN (EPUB) 978-3-11-059807-0

Library of Congress Control Number: 2018954395

Bibliographic information published by the Deutsche Nationalbibliothek
The Deutsche Nationalbibliothek lists this publication in the Deutsche Nationalbibliografie; detailed
bibliographic data are available on the Internet at http://dnb.dnb.de.

Preface: Structure and Evolution

In the twenty-first century, we highly depend on data and are part of the information society, where huge function platforms have been established by online social networks. We state our viewpoints, make friends, and interact on Twitter, Facebook, LinkedIn, Sina Microblog, WeChat, and other social networks. Lots of information generated each day are conveniently available to people. Online social activities are changing human behavior models and social formation, and social network data is becoming the most mature big data. By using the technique of big data behind every online social networks, we can hope that people's understanding on user behaviors and social phenomenon may reach an unprecedented depth.

Online social network analysis relates to computing science, sociology, management, psychology, and many other subject areas. As a chief scientist of the Major State Basic Research Development Program of China (973 Program), that is, "Fundamental Research of Social Network Analysis and Network Information Diffusion," and during my research on online social networks, I felt that this field lacked a treatise, which systematically elaborates the concepts, theories, and techniques of online social network analysis from a multidisciplinary aspect. Hence, I formed a team consisting of 973 Program, including National University of Defense Technology, Shanghai Jiao Tong University, Hefei University of Technology, Beijing University of Post & Telecommunications, Institute of Computing Technology, CAS, Peking University, University of Science and Technology Beijing, Institute of Information Engineering, CAS, and Harbin Institute of Technology. This book is a result of the research findings of these teams and a systematic review of relevant theories and techniques globally, so as to provide theoretical, systematic, and instrumental research guides for relevant researchers.

The three core factors for the analysis of online social networks are "structure and evolution," "groups and interaction," and "information and diffusion."

Volume 1 of this book consists of four chapters. Chapter 1 provides introduction for the book, followed by Chapters 2–4 that focus on the first core factor, namely, "structure and evolution." Chapter 2 is about the analysis and modeling of social network structure characteristics, Chapter 3 is about the detection techniques and approaches for virtual communities, and Chapter 4 discusses about the evolution and analysis of virtual communities.

The following experts and scholars who participated in the data collection, content arrangement, and achievement contribution of this volume are sincerely appreciated: Zhaoyun Ding, Xiaomeng Wang, Bin Wang, Yezheng Liu, Xiaodong Liu, Shenghong Li, Aiping Li, Lei Li, Shiyu Du, Peng Wu, Xiuzhen Chen, Wei Chen, Yang Yang, Lumin Zhang, Peng Shi, and Yuanchun Jiang.

Thanks to Associate Professor Shudong Li for the careful coordination and arrangement for writing this volume, and also to Weihong Han and Shuqiang Yang for reviewing and proofreading.

https://doi.org/10.1515/9783110599374-201

Contents

List of Contributors

Prof. Xueqi Cheng
Institute of Computing Technology
Chinese Academy of Sciences
No. 6 Zhongguancun Kexueyuan South Road
100190 Beijing, China

Prof. Binxing Fang
Chinese Academy of Engineering
Building A, Tri-Tower
No. 66-1 Zhongguancun East Road
100190 Beijing, China

Prof. Li Guo
Institute of Information Engineering
Chinese Academy of Sciences
No. 89 Linzhuang Road
100093 Beijing, China

Prof. Changjun Hu
University of Science and Technology Beijing
No. 30 Xueyuan Road
100083 Beijing, China

Prof. Yan Jia
National University of Defense Technology
No. 109 Deya Road, Kaifu District
410073 Changsha, China

Prof. Jianhua Li
Prof. Shanghai Jiaotong University
Software Building
No. 800 Dongchuan Road
200240 Shanghai, China

Prof. Xiangke Liao
National University of Defense Technology
No. 109 Deya Road, Kaifu District
410073 Changsha, China

Prof. Jiayin Qi
Shanghai University of International Business
and Economics
Room 338, Bocui Building
No. 1900 Wenxiang Road
201620 Shanghai, China

Prof. Xindong Wu
Hefei University of Technology
No. 193, Tunxi Road
230009 Hefei, China

Prof. Jin Xu
Peking University
No. 5 Yiheyuan Road
100871 Beijing, China

Prof. Shanlin Yang
Hefei University of Technology
No. 193, Tunxi Road
230009 Hefei, China

Prof. Hongli Zhang
Harbin Institute of Technology
No. 92 Xidazhi Street
150001 Harbin, China

Prof. Bin Zhou
National University of Defense Technology
No. 109 Deya Road, Kaifu District
410073 Changsha, China

https://doi.org/10.1515/9783110599374-202

Binxing Fang

1 Introduction

1.1 Social network and its development

1.1.1 The origin of social network

Since the beginning of mankind, people have been working together, farming and hunting, and forming a society. With the development of society and deepening of communication, various relationships are established between people. Social relationships are developed including friendships, production relationships, labor relationships, and social interactions in addition to consanguinity and familial relationships. As social members interact with other during work, study, life, entertainment, and other activities, stable relationships are gradually formed, resulting in the generation of a social network. Like Mickenberg and Dugan said in 1995, "we all connect, like a net we cannot see" [1].

In Wikipedia, social network is defined as: "a social structure made up of a set of nodes. The nodes generally refer to individuals or organizations, and the social network stands for various social relationships. In the social network, relatively stable relationship systems are formed between members due to interactions, and the relationship systems may include friendships, classmate relationships, business partnerships, or race and faith relationships. By means of these relationships, the social network ties different people closely, from those meet each other occasionally to intimate family members and then to those in various social activities" [2]. Because there are various social relationships in the social network, the social graphical structure of social organizations or individuals tends to be very complex [2]. The complex relational structure affects interactions and associations between members, affecting people's social behaviors.

From a historical perspective, social network is the backbone for integrating people and the internet. As a result of industrialization and urbanization as well as the rise of new communication technologies, society tends to be networked more and more closely. In 2012, Lee Rainie and Barry Wellman listed the social network revolution, mobile revolution, and internet revolution as the three major movements affecting human society in this era in their new book "Networked: The New Social Operating System" [3]. At present, the internet, as an interactive platform playing an important role in mutual communication, interaction, and participation, has been developed significantly beyond ARPANET's original military and technical purposes. Moreover, the social network covers almost all forms of network services centered on human society, allowing the internet to be developed from an application platform for research departments, schools, and governments/businesses into a tool for people to establish and develop relationships as well as to communicate with each other.

https://doi.org/10.1515/9783110599374-001

1.1.2 A Glimpse of the development procedure of social networks from the perspective of sociology

In 1842, French sociologist and positivism philosopher Auguste Comte (1798–1857) proposed a term [4] "sociology," defining two primary aspects of researches in sociology, i.e., social statics and social dynamics. He was the first person to propose studies on the society considering mutual relationships between social actors. Auguste Comte considered that individuals are basic elements constituting the society, while individual properties in turn exert influence on society's properties. His contributions propelled the development of sociology as a branch of science.

French sociologist Gustave Le Bon (1841–1931) claimed that the relationships [5] among social members should be observed from a group perspective, focussing on the circulation of information among group members. He pointed out that, when an individual becomes a member of a group, they lose their identity as an individual. As a member of the group, people imitate others around them. As the group's ideas and behaviors get widely spread, individuals' ideas and behaviors are deeply influenced.

From the perspective of sociology, social network originates from "Sociology" theory [6] proposed by the German sociologist Georg Simmel (1858–1918). In the 1960s, with the beginning of the Cold War and social chaos pervasive in the western world, Georg Simmel's "Sociology" theory developed rapidly in the west and became mature in the 1970s. With the development process lasting for half a century, "Social Structure" theory [7] in sociology has been widely applied in different fields including psychology, sociometric, sociology, anthropology, mathematics, statistics, and probabilism, gradually collaborating into a set of systematic theories, methods, and technology and becoming an important social structure study paradigm.

The popularity of the social networks concept originates from his description of interaction of social relationships. Over the past century, sociologists have used the metaphor of social networks to indicate various complicated social relationships. However, by the 1950, the vocabulary began to be systematically used to indicate social communities with boundaries, which are different than the traditional sense (such as villages and families), and a social category where people were regarded as separate individuals (such as gender and race). For example, considering people in a café, colleagues working together, or people communicating with each other on the internet as social communities having a boundary can lead to an erroneous belief that they have a sense of belonging to their common group because they know each other. The truth is that people keep entering or exiting from a social network, and the social network becomes a complicated structure.

In 1988, a well-known Canadian sociologist Barry Wellman proposed a relatively mature definition of social networks. He considered that the social network is a relatively stable system [8] comprising social relationships among certain individuals; that is, "network" can be regarded as a series of social connections or social relationships linking the actors, with the relatively stable relationship mode constituting the social structure. With continual expansion of the scope of application, the concept of social networks has gone beyond personal relationships; network actors may be individuals or aggregation units such as families, departments, and organizations.

The social network in its early stage mainly refers to offline social networks established among individuals through acquaintanceship or working relationships such as scientific research cooperation relationship networks and actor cooperation networks. Among these, the social relationship network of 34 members in a karate club of a university constructed by sociologist Wayne Zachary in the 1970s is a typical representation [9] of early social networks.

With the development of internet, the regional element reflected by the network structure weakened. Consequently, regional limitation in traditional offline social networks has increasingly weakened, and cross-regional online social relationships have become an important pattern of social networks. After 2003, with the emergence of Web 2.0 technology, online social network media has attracted more and more attention from people who started to create accounts on online social media platforms, typically represented by Facebook, Twitter, Blog, and other social networking sites, and add friends who they get acquainted with offline. Since then, offline social networking has expanded to network environments becoming an indispensable communication tool for people in their network life.

1.1.3 A glimpse of the development of social network from the perspective of anthropology

From the perspective of anthropology, early studies on social network mainly included two modes: nonindustrial society and industrial society.

The study on kinship by Lewis Henry Morgan (1818–1881), an American anthropologist, was the most representative of social networks in a nonindustrial society [10]. While studying the Iroquois tribes, he found that the terms of kinship terms in Iroquois were completely different from those in modern America, while the terms of kinship in other Indians was basically the same as that in Iroquois. He published a book "Systems of Consanguinity and Affinity of the Human Family" in 1871, pointing out that kinship terms were not general, and different cultures had different systems. He solved the relation problem between the culture and terms of kinship.

Alfred Radcliffe-Brown (1881–1955), an English anthropologist, inherited and developed the theory of Lewis Henry Morgan. He pointed out that the kinship system was a network of social relations composed of the network of all the social relations. Such a network of all social relations was termed the social structure. He advocated that a social network analysis method was used for analyzing the kinship relation to gradually form the structural functionalism theory [11], making social network a dominant concept in English anthropology.

However, the traditional kinship studies has two limitations: first, they only focus on individual members in the kinship relation and ignore the mutual relation among members; second, they focus on the source and historical development of the kinship and ignore the horizontal structure study. Lévi-Strauss (1908–2009), a French anthropologist, proposed a method of studying the kinship relation from a structural viewpoint [12], and summarized a binary opposition relation consisting of eight members in four groups of key relatives: husband and wife, brother and sister, father and son, and uncle and nephew. His method outlined a deep and general social network structure behind the kinship relation.

In addition to the study on the kinship relation, with colonialism collapsing and primitive society drifting away, the focus of anthropological studies shifted to wide agricultural society and social society. The study on the social relation also extended from the kinship relation to different social relations in urban cities, enterprises, and organizations. In 1929, William Lloyd Worner (1847–1928), an American anthropologist, organized the "Yankee City" project [13] to apply his method of studying Australian indigenous people to the study on American towns. He proposed a method of emphasizing social class, individual interaction, and social network. His research had a profound impact on later researchers.

Second, in the industrial society mode, the study of Max Gluckman (1911–1975), an important British anthropologist, was the most representative [14]. He observed five factories. On one hand, he continued Radcliffe-Brown's emphasis on the social structure. On the other hand, he started to focus on the wider social context where the workshop was in, treating it as the key component of the study. He found that informal organizations existed in five factories. Although the relation mode between workers and managers was different, a social relation for spontaneous cooperation did not exist; instead, numerous conflicts existed between workers and managers.

In addition to being applied to the study on the modern industrial society, the social network was applied to the study on urbanization of third-world countries. Bruce Kapferer (1940–Present), an Australian anthropologist, studied the labor conflict in a mining company [15]. Beside considering factors such as the interaction relation among workers, and the social network consisting of workers in his study, he analyzed the relation among the interaction of workers, the social network of workers, and key factory events such as strike action.

1.2 Development of online social networks

1.2.1 Concept of online social networks

With the rapid development of the Internet technology, people introduce the concept of early social networking into the Internet, and create the online social networks for social networking services (SNS). The meaning of online social networks includes hardware, software, service, and application. Because a word group consisting of four words meets Chinese's word-formation habit, people customarily use the social network to replace the SNS.

The online social networks can be divided into four categories according to the research report [16] on social computing of European Union:

(1) Instant messaging applications, which are platforms for providing online real-time communication, such as MSN, QQ, AIM, Fetion and WeChat, and have mutual authentication and real-time push characteristics;

(2) Online social applications, which are platforms for providing online social relationships, such as Facebook, Google+ (Google), RENN, Kaixin001 and Qzone, and have mutual authentication and non-realtime access characteristics;

(3) Microblog-type applications, which are platforms for bi-directionally releasing short messages, such as Twitter, Sina weibo, Tencent weibo, and NetEase weibo and Sohu weibo, and have one-way authentication and realtime push characteristics;

(4) Space-sharing type applications, which are Web 2.0 applications which can communicate with each other but are not tightly combined, such as forums, blogs, BBS, video sharing, social bookmark and online shopping, and have one-way authentication and non-realtime access characteristics.

The online social network is a social structure made up of a set of social actors and a set of ties between these actors in the information network. This social structure mainly includes three factors, including relationship structure, network groups and network information. The relationship structure of the social network is a network system formed via the connection of individual members of the society. Individuals are also referred to as nodes, and can be regarded as organizations, individuals, network ID, other entity or virtual individual with different meanings; however, the relationship between individuals can be family relations, movement behavior, send and receive messages and a variety of other relationships. Based on these relationships, the individuals in the social network self-organize a variety of virtual communities. The virtual community is a subset of social networks, and has a close connection between the nodes in the virtual community, and a sparse connection between the nodes of different virtual communities. On the basis of the relationships above, various information is transferred between the individuals, between an individual and a group, and between the groups in the social network. The constant iteration process of this information transfer is information spreading in the social network. Due to the influences of the network structure and the information transfer, individuals cluster or get together in a certain virtual community for a certain event, affect, act and rely on each other, and purposefully act in a similar manner. This forms a group behavior of the social network.

The social network is a typical application of the Web 2.0 era, and is also a typical representative of sociality and initiative characteristics of the Web 2.0 era. The Internet of the Web 2.0 era is undergoing great change—from a series of websites to mature service platforms that provide network applications for final users [17]. The contents in these platforms are produced due to the participation of each user; and personalized contents produced due to participation form current Web 2.0 world via people-to-people sharing. The social websites, such as Facebook and Twitter, are the masterpieces of the initiative participation of users in the Web 2.0 era. Facebook has been on the line for less than 8 years, and has owned more than 1,400 million users; and Twitter also has more than 500 million users. According to the report of each official website, until March 2013, the number of Sina Weibo users has exceeded 556 million.

Along with the incoming peak period of Web 2.0 applications, Web 3.0 also starts to emerge. Father of the Internet, Tim Berners-Lee, indicated [18] that when the Internet develops into a semantic network covering a large number of data, people can access the incredible data resource, i.e., Web 3.0. In the network summit on 16 November 2010, Mary Meeker indicated that Web 3.0 is made up of "Social Networking, Mobile and Search" [19]. In conclusion, the characteristics of Web 3.0 include: converting the Internet into a database, making a search engine intelligent, achieving the semantic network and the service-oriented architecture (SOA), and converting the Internet into a series of three-dimensional space (such as people, time and information). It can be said that who can lead Web 3.0, and who is the next actor of the network.

1.2.2 Features of online social networks

Compared with traditional Web and information media applications, the online social networks mainly have the following new features.
(1) Immediacy: Information can be released and received easily and quickly. A user can release and receive information over a phone or browser at any time from any place.
(2) Spreadability: "Nuclear fission" type information dissemination. Once released, a message will be immediately pushed to all followers by the system, and as long as being reposted, it will be disseminated to a new batch of followers at once. Thus, a "nuclear fission" type geometric spread trend is presented and opinion spread channels are created for ordinary people.
(3) Equality: Everyone stands a chance to become an opinion leader. Compared with asymmetric information release and info receiver in traditional media, all users of social network services stand a chance to form opinion leadership over social networks, and thus play important roles in occurrence, development, spread, discussion stages of emergency events.

(4) Self-organization: They appear in the form of We Media and can quickly form virtual communities. That's because individuals in social networks all have their own means and channels to provide and release information, and can quickly form online virtual communities by means of fast information dissemination of the social networks.

1.2.3 Development of online social networks

In a certain sense, online social networks are derived from people's demands for social activities over networks. Figure 1.1 illustrates the development history of online social networks. In 1838, Samuel F.B. Morse invented the Morse code, and then the telegram became a long-distance communication channel; this makes online real-time long-distance communication over social networks possible. In 1876, Bell invented a line switching mode that can be used in telecommunication networks, and thus the first practical telephone was officially produced. In 1969, ARPANET was invented in America. The first packet switched network in the world was then formally operated. In 1971, the first E-mail was sent by a researcher of Advanced

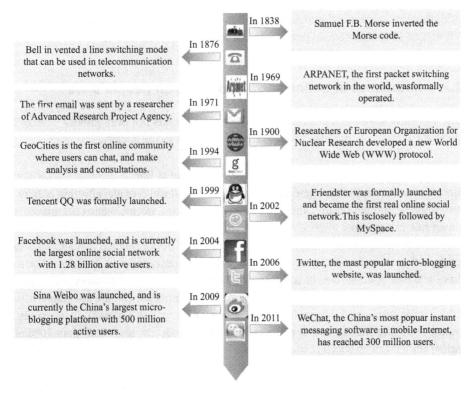

Figure 1.1: Development history of online social networks.

Research Project Agency. In 1990, a researcher of European Organization for Nuclear Research developed a new World Wide Web (WWW) protocol, which marked the official birth of modern Internet. In 1994, Yahoo! GeoCities became the first Internet online community, where users can chat, make analysis and consultations. In 1999, Tencent QQ was launched. In 2002, Friendster was launched and became the first real online social network. In 2004, Facebook was launched. It now has developed to be the biggest online social network and already has 128 million active users by March 2014. In 2006, Twitter, the most popular microblogging website, was launched. It is one of top ten most visited Internet websites. Later, Sina Weibo and other domestic social networks were successively launched, which marked the further expansion and maturity of social networks.

Currently, social network applications are blooming. Based on a survey by Adobe, Facebook, which has been set up for more than 10 years, ranks first in top ten social networks by January 2014. It has about 1,400 million registered users and thus is called the third "populous nation". Most of the registered users are from America, up to about 160 million, and what followed are users from Brazil, India, Indonesia, Mexico, Turkey, and Britain. Now, Facebook has 1,000 million monthly active mobile users. YouTube ranks second, having more than 1,000 million users. Chinese QQ Space and Sina Weibo, respectively having 623 million users and 556 million users, rank third and fourth. Following by are Twitter, Google+, LinkedIn, VKontakte (a Russian social network), Chinese RENN, WeChat in turn.

1.2.4 Influences of online social networks on people's life

The vigorous development of online social networks has not only greatly changed people's way of life, but also brought negative effects to the society.

1. Online social networks have changed people's way of life

Online social networks have gradually penetrated into all walks of life, affecting politics, education, economy, culture, and other aspects. In politics, microblogging has played a direct role in a number of government activities. In 2008, Obama had used Twitter for election activities, and his campaign team had moulded public opinion in microblogs to compete for votes. In education, more than 50 famous universities in the United States have released open classes in social networks to directly support distance education. Open classes are offered in Facebook and Twitter communities, and are integrated with educational resources such as MOOCs (Massive Open Online Courses). In economy, online shopping has become a mainstream way of shopping, and more than 70% of active adult users on social networks choose to shop online. Companies including Cole, Target and Ford have greatly improved their brand awareness by marketing on Facebook, and their turnover has increased by 10%. In culture, online social networks have changed people's way of life. Netizens can make friends, play games, and interact and cooperate with others without going out, and thus the so called "indoorsy life" is formed. In terms of social interaction and communication, social networks are sure to bring "social dividend" to conventional banks. The great potential of social networks allows domestic banks to develop strategies focusing on finding new profit growth points by using the social networks. Now in China, a WeChat Bank has been established under the cooperation of the China Merchants Bank with WeChat which is an emerging tool, to provide more convenient services to users with the help of WeChat, and this will also facilitate the application of WeChat to a broader field.

2. Online social networks have brought negative effects to the society

Online social networks have also brought negative effects to the society while facilitating people's lives. In politics, some perpetrators deliberately create and spread rumors that are detrimental to national interests to affect social stability. For example, in 2011, the perpetrators incited the riots in London and other cities by using Facebook, and a "Rob Salt Tide" appeared in China because people were deluded by rumors on microblogging, which greatly affected the social stability. In education, evil forces educate young people to advocate violence and preach destructive individual heroism through social networks. In economy, perpetrators release false information through chat tools and cheat customers through online shopping platforms. In culture, vulgar gangs disseminate online pornography and violent video content by means of social videos, instant messaging and other channels. In life, private information in social networks which make information transparent would be easily misused by undesirables, and as a result, people's normal life will be disturbed.

In terms of public opinion, event propagation on social networks contributes greatly to effects of public opinion. But adverse public opinion will have a huge impact on social stability. On 15 February 2011, riots broke out in Benghazi, Libya. Anti-government groups communicated with each other through Facebook and then set up a "liberal alliance", calling on people to join the anti-government forces, which had up to 15000 followers. On October 20, the Libyan leader Muammar Gaddafi was shot to death by the anti-government forces. Social networks played a role in fueling the early riots in Libya.

We can see from the facts given above that the essence of social networks is to help form public opinion quickly, to influence people's thinking, affect people's world view, epistemic notions, values, and philosophy of life. In social networks, it is simple and convenient to release and receive information, every one has the right to speak online, various topics and views concerning national economy and the people's livelihood can be released at any time, and information can be spread in a way just like "nuclear fission" and may be overstated by opinion leaders to promote establishment of virtual communities for those having the same ideas and aspirations, and the masses can be organized and aroused quickly to participate in social activities, so a social mobilization force is formed.

1.3 Background and significance of online social network analysis

Social network analysis relates to a calculable analysis method, which integrates theories and methods of informatics, mathematics, sociology, management, psychology, and other sciences and is provided to understand formation of different social relationships, behavior characteristic analysis, and information dissemination laws. Social network analysis was first put forward by a well-known British anthropologist Radcliffe-Brown in his analysis and research on social structures. He appealed to carry out systematical research and analysis on social networks [20]. With deepening analysis on social networks by sociologists, anthropologists, physicists, mathematicians, especially mathematicians in graph theory, and statisticians, the theories, methods, and techniques formed in social network analysis have become an important social structure research paradigm. Thanks to online social networks' features of large scale, dynamism, anonymity, rich contents and data, etc., in recent years, analysis and research on emerging online social networks, such as social websites, blogs, and Weibo, have been flourishing, and play a decisive role in social structure research.

Social network analysis can function in many aspects, including political election, marketing, criminal chase, etc.

"Obama's victory in the United States presidential election of 2008" is a typical case of political election. On September 2008, Obama campaign created a social network analysis team to win the election. The team set up a donor database, an opinion poll database, and a network database. They grouped neutral electors based on their races, occupations, and other features, and then expressed different political propositions regarding different groups via emails, for example, they expressed propositions against racial discrimination for the black, expressed propositions on improving treatment for doctors, and expressed propositions on protecting workers' rights for building workers. These efforts produced a dramatical effect. On November 2008, according to data published by Gallup, the approval rate of Obama exceeds that of McCain by 11% points, and Obama finally won that election. If it's just a trial in 2008, then Obama got familiar with the social network analysis in the election of 2012. Someone even call Obama as the first "social network president" [21].

"Amazon recommendation system" is a typical case of marketing. Amazon is an American e-commerce company, on which people can shop, and books are its major products. The early Amazon recommendation system uses the approach of manual recommendation. But now, Amazon uses an automated recommendation system. The system first collects information of people on Amazon's website, including purchase history, browsing behavior, goods reviews, favorites contents of customers, then classifies customers with similar information into one group based on the information, and finally recommends goods to other users based on purchase of users from the same group. Application of the system improves Amazon's sales amount by 35%.

American LWAS information company, providing social media strategy consultation for the law enforcement agencies, says: "criminals will leave traces everywhere they went—in their cell phones, in their Twitter accounts, or in their Facebook". These traces can provide important clues for the law enforcement officers from both basic-level police departments and top government agencies when they search for criminals on social medial websites, such as Facebook, Myspcase, Twitter, and YouTube [22, 23]. For example, New York Police Department set a Facebook special detachment to explore crime clues from social media [24].

1.4 Scientific questions of online social network analysis

1.4.1 Challenges of online social network analysis

An online social network has three central elements: first is its network structure, second is its group interaction, and finally the information dissemination. The three dimensions cover a wide range and involve several academic disciplines, such as informatics, mathematics, and management science. Therefore, the core of online social network analysis can be summarized as three elements: "Relationship structure", "Network groups" and "Network information". As illustrated in Figure 1.2, the three elements are correlated and interdependent: the "relationship structure" provides an underlying platform to network group interaction behaviors, and is the carrier of a social network; the "network groups" directly promote dissemination of network information and affect the relationship structure in turn, and are the subjects of the social network; and the "network information" and its dissemination are prerequisites of the social network, are also inducements and effects of group behaviors, can affect the change of the relationship structure, and are the objects of the social network.

Since the study on the nature of large-scale social networks and the basic law of network information dissemination is still in a relatively primary stage, complete fundamental theories and methods on social networks and their information dissemination have not been proposed yet. For the three central elements, there are still a number of problems that are not clearly understood, and many challenges are waiting ahead.

Challenge I: The structure of an online social network is characterized in mass nodes, structural complexity, multi-dimensional evolution, etc. Specifically speaking,

Mass nodes: Facebook has more than 1.28 billion active users all over the world, and is the "third most populous nation" [25].

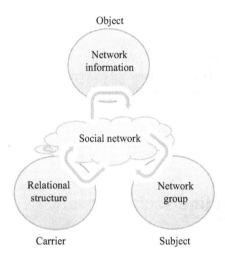

Figure 1.2: Relationship structure, network groups and network information in a social network.

Structural complexity: there are various relationships among 536 million users of Sina Weibo, including concern/fans, mention, and forward.

Multi-dimensional evolution: in a community of Twitter for discussing infectious diseases, evolving topics are complex and diverse within 30 days [26].

Challenge II: Group interaction in online social networks has the characteristics of strong interactive evolution, public emotional upheaval, etc. The standpoints of the public are changing and their points of interest are evolving. Specifically speaking,

Group clustering: a plurality of Twitter users published false information, raising the public panic event that a large number of migrant workers flee Mumbai, Bangalore, Chennai and other cities [27].

Strong interactivity: in the community consisting of Sina Weibo users, the interactive relationships include mention, reply, concern/fans, and other direct relationships.

Emotional variability: people are most positive at breakfast time of a day; after lunch, people get depressed gradually; and before bedtime, people's emotions rise sharply [28].

Challenge III: Information dissemination of online social networks has the characteristic of multisource concurrence, and the mutual influence makes the paths variable and content evolutionary. Specifically speaking,

Multisource concurrence: For example, Kai-Fu Lee registered accounts on multiple social network platforms, and then published information on the multiple platforms concurrently.

Mutual influence: KLM Royal Dutch Airlines used social media for marketing communication, and achieved good results through the mutual influence between Twitter users [29].

Content evolution: in the Egyptian revolution, within an hour after the former President Hosni Mubarak announced that he would step down, the topic "Jan25" on Twitter spread and evolved so fast [30].

1.4.2 Three scientific questions and associated researches

Regarding the aforementioned three challenges, from three new perspectives, i.e., "structure and evolution", "group and interaction", and "information and dissemination", we have generalized in this book corresponding three scientific questions during online social network analysis, which are mainly reflected in three aspects: property and evolution mechanism of social network structure, formation and interaction law of social network group behaviors, and social network information dissemination law and evolution mechanism.

(1) Scientific question I: Property and evolution mechanism of online social network structures.
How are the structures of social networks represented? What kind of representation method can reflect the essence of social networks while support computation and analysis at the same time? What kind of computation method can accurately depict the evolution of social network structures?

(2) Scientific question II: Formation and interaction law of online social network community behaviors.
How can the existence and formation methods of groups be depicted in social networks? How can the interactive influence among groups be represented and measured? How should the influence exerted by the interactive process among groups on the evolution of communities be computed?

(3) Scientific question III: Online social network information dissemination law and evolution mechanism.
How can the connotation of information be represented in a computable way? What are the methods for computing the dissemination process and status of information on social networks? How is the computation method used to depict mutual influence between information connotation and information dissemination?

Hereinafter, we will expound major issues and contents involved in the three scientific questions.

1. Structure and evolution – properties and evolution mechanisms of social network structures

"Structure and evolution" corresponds to the first scientific question, i.e., properties and evolution mechanisms of social network structures. In this part, issues in three key aspects are to be solved, which are social network structure analysis and modeling, discovery of virtual communities in social network, as well as the evolution law of social networks.

1) Social network structure analysis and modeling

Social network structure analysis and modeling serve as the basis for all analysis. Social network structure analysis refers to analyzing many statistical properties through a statistical analysis method, including the distribution law of node degrees in a network, the intimacy degree of relationships, the intimacy degree of acquaintance relationship, the importance of a certain user for message delivery with all other users in the network. Social network modeling refers to adopting a structure modeling methods regarding the properties of social networks to study the mechanisms generating these properties, so as to deeply understand the inner law and essential characteristics of social networks.

The well-known Weak Ties theory studies social networks from the perspective of structure. Even famous examples in network structure studies are researches on small-world property [31] in 1998 and discovery of scale-free property [32] in 1999. The researches have greatly boosted the development in the network research field, and initiated a new trend in network researches. In recent years, the development of online social networks has driven people to search for its complicated inner mechanisms eagerly. Social network structures reflect relationships between individuals in social networks. Full understanding of social network structures provides support for other studies on scientific questions of social networks and lays the foundation for establishing basic theories and analysis methods for social networks. These important scientific questions include user impact analysis, studies on community interaction mechanism, information dissemination and evolution analysis, community discovery as well as studies on community formation mechanism . As the mobile Internet era arrives, the scale of users in online social networks grows with each passing day. Tens of millions of users as well as a growing number make it infeasible to represent social network structures through visualized methods. The ordinary research method is depicting network structures by virtue of network statistical characteristics; as a result, network structures can be learned through researches on different network characteristics.

The significance of social network structure analysis and modeling lies on the one hand in generating, when it is difficult to get the real network, an analog network for replacing the real network to conduct researches, and the other hand in exploring the method and mechanism for generating a specific network structure. Therefore, social network structure analysis and social network structure modeling are two primary methods in social network structure studies, and are inseparable from each other. Network statistical property guide network structure modeling, and serve as a yardstick for the structure modeling method. In addition, the structure modeling process also discloses the inner mechanism of corresponding network statistical property. Therefore, the establishment of the social network structure model not only provides us with a replacement of the real social network, but also enables us to explore the generation mechanism of the real social network. The researches on social network structures serve as the foundation for social network researches. The continual development of this research field greatly propels the progress of social network science, or even the complex network science.

2) Virtual communities and discovery technology
Virtual community discovery is a must-have function for social network analysis. In the field of sociology, community refers to a personal relationship network [33] formed by a group of people who engage in public discussions on the network and who have a deep relationship with each other after a period of time. The phenomenon that relationships are uneven exists in the social network; the relationships among some individuals are intimate while some relationships are estranged; as a result, a community form having closer relationships is formed by centering on a certain focus on a certain a regular community, and the community form can be considered as a virtual community structure in social networks. Virtual community structure refers to a typical topological structure feature of the online social network. In online social networks, such as Sina Weibo and Facebook, the condition of close relationships among users can be found by digging the community, so as to obtain social relationships among users as well as social characters of the users; and by further combining analysis on users' viewpoints/behaviors and so on in the community, it is easier to understand network topological structure characteristics, disclose inner function characteristics of a complex system, and understand individual relationship/behavior in the community as well as the evolution trend.

Virtual community structures tend to disclose various connotations, such as modules, categories, groups, and teams. Various complex networks can be abstracted as graph structures in mathematics; therefore, many scholars and researchers are trying to describe and depict the community structures by virtue of the mathematical tool, and provide their respective discovery methods [34] from different perspectives. In essence, the discovery of the virtual community in online social networks is the process of dividing network nodes into several sub-graphs according to the close connection degree of their inner topological structures. During the early stage of discovering algorithm researches in the community, people defined some global target functions for measuring network community structure strength, and designed algorithms to optimize these functions to discover the community structure. The network data structure scale in the early stage was relatively small; understanding of the community structure is relatively onefold; and the requirement for time complexity of algorithms is not so high, either. With the development of online social networks, the processing technology of social network big data brings new opportunities and challenges for community discovery; and how to rapidly discover the virtual community structure and analyze hierarchy and overlapping of the community structure in heterogeneous and multi-dimensional social networks is a key research issue of group management control on a rapidly changing network era.

As a meso structure in social networks, the virtual community not only reflects high dynamism of the network on a micro level, but also reflects stability of the network on a macro level; this feature is a research basis for the formation and evolution mechanism of the virtual community in social networks. With the vigorous development of online social networks, analyzing large-scale network data to discover virtual communities present therein can facilitate understanding structural constitution of network virtual society and can also prevent and reduce many illegal behaviors that threat network security. In addition, the discovery of network virtual communities further exerts important influence on dynamical behaviors on the network. For example, the present of virtual community structures in online social networks exerts immense influence on message dissemination. Therefore, in the online social network environment, analyzing and discovering the virtual community structures present in the environment play an important role in understanding structural characteristics of network stratification organization, categorization of node individuals, as well as various network properties and dynamic behaviors.

3) Analysis on virtual community evolution

A virtual community has dynamical evolution property; and it is necessary to analyze and identify the evolution mechanism. Virtual community structures reflect local aggregation features of individual behaviors in the network; these virtual community structures are not constant; because online social network structures keep evolving over time, virtual community structures also undergo continuous evolution. A large number of various explicit or implicit virtual community structures exist in online social networks, such as circles on renren.com and teams on douban.com, which keep evolving dynamically and continuously. The evolution of virtual communities is closely related to the functions of social networks in such aspects as diffusion, anti-disaster, cooperation, and synchronization, and also plays a fundamental role in the evolution of the social networks.

In fact, the change from static network analysis to researches on the evolution of dynamic networks is a new trend of social network researches in recent years. With the advent of the big data era, obtaining and analyzing large-scale dynamic network evolution data are made possible, which provides an important basis for evolution analysis of dynamic network virtual communities. In recent years, researches have focused on the evolution issues [35] of social network dynamic virtual communities mainly from three aspects. The first aspect is the mechanism for the emergency of virtual communities or the reason for the formation of virtual communities; how is the emerging process of virtual communities restored or modeled according to these mechanisms. The next is which factors have exerted influence on the evolution process of virtual communities after the formation of them; because online social network structures and evolution process are complicated with many influencing factors, how to dig out the key factors during the evolution of virtual communities has become an important and challenging topic in researches. Existing researches mainly concentrate on the influence of three key factors on the evolution of virtual communities, i.e., accumulative effect of user individuals, structural diversity and structural equilibrium. After the formation reason of virtual communities and factors influencing the evolution are realized, the discovery algorithms of dynamic virtual communities can be researched then, i.e., how to identify the whole sequences of evolved virtual communities in dynamic networks.

The evolution of social network virtual communities is closely related to network functions, and closely affects dissemination of information on social networks and also plays a fundamental role in the evolution of social networks. As a result, researches on the evolution and analysis of virtual communities are of vital importance. Besides, the influence of other behaviors in online social networks on evolution dynamics of virtual communities, such as information dissemination, artificial control, emergency events, and other factors in online social networks, attracts more and more attention from people. As the big data era arrives, researches on these aspects will also enter a phase featured by rapid development.

2. Group and interaction: Group behavior formation and interaction in social networks

"Group and interaction" corresponds to the second scientific question, namely, group behavior formation and interaction in social networks. This scientific question mainly deals with user behavior analysis, network sentiment analysis and individual influence analysis in social networks as well as key issues in collective aggregation and mechanisms that influence it. It mainly includes user behavior analysis, social network sentiment analysis and individual influence analysis as well as analysis on collective aggregation and mechanisms that influence it.

1) User behavior analysis

User individual behavior is the basic action in the community and needs to be modeled. User behavior in online social networks includes self-display, building relationships with strangers, sharing interests and information, releasing, searching, browsing and pushing information; interacting with different people based on various topics; and building interest community, learning and entertainment community, sharing knowledge, study and communication, and sharing happiness.

User behavior is an important research part of online social networks. User behavior in social networks is the willingness of users to make use of social network services on the basis of a comprehensive evaluation on their own needs, social impact and social network technologies, and a variety of use activities resulted therefrom. The research on user behavior in online social networks is mainly based on the following two ideas: using online social networks as a specific information technology, and studying users' adoption and denial behavior and loyalty to the online social network technology; considering online social networks as a platform for providing various services and applications, and studying the characteristics and regularities that users use various services and applications. Considering online social networks as a specific information technology, researchers explore the effects of demographic variables, individuality traits, and emotional, cognitive and motivational factors as well as social, physical and technological environment on users' adoption and loyalty to online social networks by using classical theories of behavioral study such as Technology Acceptance Model, Theory of Planned Behavior, Expectation Confirmation Theory, and Flow Experience Theory. Regarding online social networks as a platform for providing a variety of services and applications, researchers conduct studies on individual usage behaviors such as self-presentation, micro-blog release, search, browse and comment, and user group interaction behaviors such as relationship establishment and content selection so as to reveal the underlying mechanism of content creation behavior and content consumption behavior in online social networks.

User behavior is the external performance of user motivation. Mastering the characteristics and regularities of user behavior in social networks to analyze the internal mechanism of user behavior in online social networks helps providers of online social network services to innovate social network service models, and helps to provide a theoretical basis for the monitoring and intervention of network public opinion.

2) Social network sentiment analysis
Sentiment analysis (aka opinion mining in this book) is a process of analysis, processing and induction of subjective information (positive, negative or neutral). Subjective information shows user's emotion or sentiment orientation. In social networks, everyone has different influences due to different emotional states.

Although many researchers realized the importance of sentiment analysis, techniques for sentiment analysis developed slowly before 1990s. One important reason is that the available data for analysis is very limited. With the rise of Internet, the Internet has become an important media for people to obtain information. Massive online news and reports are available for researchers to study sentiment analysis. Sentiment analysis has developed rapidly in the field of natural language processing. With the rise of Web 2.0 and social networks, users can express their views and opinions on online social media at any moment, which contribute massive corpus for sentiment analysis as well as bringing many new problems and challenges. Compared with news and reports, documents in social networks are short in length with irregular grammar. Besides, there are a large number of noise data as well as popular Internet slang. All these characters make sentiment analysis more difficult. At the same time, group characteristics in social networks and link and interaction among groups also bring a new research field to traditional sentiment analysis (the previous main resources for sentiment analysis are news and reports). Techniques of semantic-based sentiment analysis and supervised learning based sentiment analysis are gradually formed. At present, sentiment analysis has involved in many research areas such as natural language processing, short text mining and Web data mining, playing an important role in management science and sociology.

Sentiment analysis is an important part of social network analysis, and it is widely used in areas of product comments, public sentiment control and information prediction. Sentiment analysis provides users with an emotional summary of historical evaluation, which enables users to quickly understand the product's evaluation information. In the public opinion monitor area, various topics and views related to national interest and people's livelihood can be released at any time. The interaction between virtual social networks and the real society increases direct impact on society, which directly affects national security and social stability. Analysis on people's emotions and attitudes in the network will play a very important role in maintaining national stability and promoting social development.

3) Individual influence analysis

Individual influence analysis is an important part of social network analysis. Individual social influence can be reflected through social activities among users, for example, the behavior and thought of users are changed under the influence of other people. In today's online social era, social networks have been a significant impact on people's daily life and behavior, a small number of malicious users and opinion leaders take advantage of social network services to make and disseminate public opinions. Opinion leaders make interaction between the media and Internet users for public opinion, and their views tend to affect a large number of fans and public opinion.

With the emergence of a large number of online social network services and user's participation, the relevant research on the individual influence analysis in social networks has attracted the attention of large number of scholars both at home and abroad. Since Katz and Lazarsfeld found that social influence plays an important role in social life and decision making in the 1950s [36], influence analysis has been widely used in a number of areas, such as recommendation systems, social network information dissemination, link prediction, viral marketing, public health, expert discovery, incident detection and advertising, etc.. Early work explored and analyzed the performance and related factors of influence in social activities, and made an in-depth study on the function model and generation mechanism of social influence. Many social phenomena related to influence and their underlying principles have been discovered. However, at that time, the sample space for the study was small, and the available data was limited. A large number of objective data was needed. With the popularity of online social networks, social network large data has brought new opportunities and challenges. How to find high influence users in heterogeneous, multi-attribute social networks, and to analyze the influence intensity among users in social networks, is a research focus for the information decision in the fast-changing network age. At present, in social networks, individual influence analysis mainly includes the analysis of the influence intensity among users and the discovery of the influence individual. Therefore, how to find high influence users in heterogeneous, multi-attribute social networks, and to analyze the influence intensity among users in social networks, is a key problem.

Because network individuals in social networks gradually turn into the state that a few become opinion leaders and most follow the crowd, the study on the individual influence in social networks has important theoretical value and practical significance. The opinion leaders can take advantage of social network services to make and disseminate public opinions. The opinion leaders make interaction between the media and Internet users for public opinion, and their views tend to affect a large number of fans and public opinion. The opinion leaders play an important role in participation and guidance. In addition, influence analysis is widely used in a number of areas, such as recommendation systems, social network information dissemination, link prediction, viral marketing, public health, expert discovery, incident detection and advertising etc.

4) Analysis on collective aggregation and mechanisms that influence it

A group in online social networks is a virtual community. Collective aggregation is usually triggered by specific incentives. Many individuals in the real society gradually join and interact with each other to form a closely related community. A group shares information and interacts with other members through online social networks, and the individuals in the group can influence each other. Consequently, the Web 2.0 world is full of countless virtual groups with different sizes, various purposes, and dynamic variations. Although some online virtual groups are based on geographical distribution, most of them have no geographical restrictions, which is a distinct difference from the traditional concept of a group.

The study on groups has been a hot issue of sociology, psychology, economics, and management science. Since The Crowd (Gustave Le Bon) was published [37] in 1897, scholars have sought an in-depth understanding of groups, especially group behavior. Every economic phenomenon, political decision or social transformation undoubtedly results from collective power. With the rapid development of the Internet, the network is increasingly showing a trend of integration between the real society and the virtual society. The biggest feature is that members of society become the subject of the Internet. At present, the collective aggregation and mechanisms that influence it in social networks mainly focus on collective aggregation mechanism, modeling method and evolution rules, followed by mining and constructing a group evolution behavior model through analysis on behavioral and psychological motivation and influence factors of the social network group to reveal the inherent mechanism of social network group evolution. On the basis of these features, online social networks are more likely to engender some extreme collective aggregation behaviors: group intelligence and group polarization. Briefly, group intelligence is a group behavior in which many individuals generate problem-solving ability superior to their own through mechanisms such as competition and cooperation, differentiation and integration, and feedback and selection. Group polarization refers to the effect of discussions among group members on individual members' opinions or decisions in group decision-making situations, which leads to behavioral consistency within groups. In the past two years, Diggle (Tony Diggle, 2013) et al. showed how group intelligence can help in finding a solution to the global scarcity of water [38]. David (David H. Zhu, 2013) et al. applied polarization to decision making in business or company seminars [39]. They are both topics with great theoretical and practical values, which deserves further exploration.

The analysis on collective aggregation and mechanisms that influence it is of great significance for the monitoring and guidance to public emergencies. A great amount of network events show that after a public emergency occurs, when traditional media has not reported it yet or keeps silent, network media reports it in the first time and tracks the latest developments to quickly attract the audiences' attention. When Internet users browse the relevant information on the Internet, they will express their opinions and interact with others by means of follow-up comments or instant comments. A lot of manpower and time are required for organization and communication in reality; however, network group behavior can usually form a large scale in a short time.

3. Information and communications-Information communications regularity in social network and evolution mechanism

"Information and communications" corresponds to the third scientific question: information communications regularity in social network and evolution mechanism. This scientific question mainly solves problems in terms of information retrieval in online social network, information communications regularity in social network, topic discovery and evolution, and influence maximization calculation method.

1) Information retrieval in online social network

Information retrieval refers to the process of finding materials (which are usually documents) meeting user information requirements from the set (which is usually saved in a computer) of massive unstructured data (which is usually in a form of text) [40]. In addition to search systems which are similar to us and representative of Google, the information retrieval system includes a classification system, recommender system, question answering system, etc. With the rapid popularization and development of the social network, information retrieval creates new resources and opportunities, and also faces new problems and challenges. The method of obtaining information for the emerging resource, social network, attracts broad attention of industry and academic field.

Facing information retrieval in online social network is an important study. Massive information is generated in social networks representative of Weibo every day. At present, a large variety of emergent events, news, and powerful topics have been reported via the social networks. The social network plays an important role in some great events (such as earthquake and aviation accident). It can quickly gather information from different organizations and propagate it to users. In addition, celebrity and friend effects in the social network give good support to information propagation. Even some products have good sales via the social network. Currently, related technology facing information retrieval in social network covers three aspects of content retrieval, classification, and social recommendation, is initially applied to different social networks, and produces user values and product commercial values. Compared with the traditional Web page, the social network document has limitations on text words, is required to be expressed in a particular way, and includes the social relation information of the author and among authors. These differences make it difficult for the traditional information retrieval technology to be directly applied to the social network. The current work is to explore and analyze authors, topics, and hyperlink information in the social network, and study the short text feature and communications mechanism in the social network, thus discovering many ways of improving content retrieval, classification, and social recommendation. But the social network is developing and changing, the present work is not fully practical. How to perfectly apply information such as the author, the relation network of authors, forwarding and replying, and hyperlink to the existing method is a key study. Therefore, there're still many problems and difficulties for retrieval of the social network. The study on retrieval provides academic values and application values.

There're many differences between information retrieval in online social network and traditional information retrieval. The features of the former one bring challenges and opportunities for the traditional information retrieval. The study on the information retrieval technology of the social network can not only provide better experience for users but also get the latest information so as to provide the theoretical basis for public decision and public opinion guidance. Moreover, it can promote communications and propagation of political, economical, and cultural activities, and offer important social values and application values.

2) Information communications regularity in social network

Information communications is an activity for delivering, receiving, and feeding back information via symbols and signals, and is a process of exchanging opinions, ideas, and emotions by people to know and effect each other [41]. Social network information communications specifies the information communications process made via the social network medium. Born by its flexibility and openness, the online social network gradually becomes an important center where information is propagated in modern society. The information communications in the social network becomes active to an unprecedented degree.

The rapid development of the social network provides rich data basis for researchers so that they have opportunities to study the information communications mechanism and know the information communications regularity on the basis of massive true data. Currently, the social network information communications mainly involves the network structure, community in network, and the propagated information. Related work is made on the basis of these factors. In terms of the information propagation model, the network structure-based research result mainly includes the independent cascade model, linear threshold model, and extension model; the community-based research result mainly includes the infectious propagation model and influence propagation model; and the information feature-based research result mainly includes the multi-source information propagation model, information competition propagation model, etc. In terms of popularity prediction, information such as the popularity trend, final popularity, and short popularity of the network content is predicted. The earliest method is mainly based on the historical popularity and user behaviors. In order to improve the prediction precision, researchers have proposed a propagation process and network structure-based method in recent years. In terms of information tracing, tracing is a technical means of widely collecting information in the social network and tracking the particular information to find the initial site or user who publishes the information, and the information propagation path. The representative method includes a centrality measurement-based tracing method and a statistical reasoning framework-based tracing method. In addition, for multi-source concurrency and incomplete observation, researchers have proposed a back propagation and node partition-based multi-source information tracing technology.

The study on the information communications regularity in social network can help us understand the social network and social phenomenon, and make us aware the topology structure, propagation capability, and dynamics behaviors of the complicated network. Moreover, it is helpful in model discovery, influential node identification, and personalized recommendation. The research result has wide applications to information recommendation of marketing and shopping sites, and public opinion monitoring and guidance. In terms of social benefits, social organizations and government organizations can publish information based on the information propagation features and regularity to improve management efficiency and transparency, and filter information to reasonably guide public. Therefore, the study on the information communications regularity in social network has theoretical values and application values.

3) Topic discovery and evolution

In the study on the social network, the topic refers to an influential event or activity, or all related events and activities. Events or activities refer to things happened in the particular time and place. News and events in each time moment, place, and language are reported in the social network, and propagated online without geographical boundary.

Topic discovery and evolution are important studies in mining of network texts. The TDT (Topic Detection and Tracking) project [42] initiated by the Defense Advanced Research Projects Agency (DARPA) defined and illustrated the topic discovery and evolution comprehensively. The topic discovery and evolution refer to discovery of texts with the same topic in news at the very beginning, and generally use a clustering method. However, with the development of the social network, the traditional topic discovery and evolution can't adapt to the current network environment. We need to find a new method and way to complete such task. First, topic discovery and evolution in the social network do not only focus on news texts; instead, Blog, Weibo, etc. become research objects. Second, compared with the traditional text, the text in the social network has its distinctive features such as short Weibo, frequent use of Internet slangs, and informal words. These features make it urgent for us to use a new analysis method or improve the existing method to improve the analysis result. At present, the study on the topic discovery includes two types. One is to preset a topic that is to be monitored and detect whether this topic appears in the social network. The other one is to monitor the new topic that appears in the social network. How to extract the topic that interests users from massive, dynamic, and multi-source social network data, recommend it, track the development and change in the topic, and get the event trend is a key study on the information decision in the rapidly changing network times. Different from the topic discovery and evolution in the traditional media, as a new research topic, the topic discovery and evolution in the social network are not deeply studied and explored. The study on the topic discovery and evolution is still at early stages.

With the development of the social network, we shift our attention to the network. Network space becomes a new site where we publish messages, propagate message, and know information. Therefore, analyzing the network information, especially information in the social network to find the topic and events, knowing the occurrence and evolution of an online topic are valuable and meaningful for enterprises to carry out targeted network marketing, and for the government to perform multi-granularity public opinion monitoring.

4) Influence maximization

Influence maximization is a key research focus in the field of information propagation in the social network, and has the purpose of discovering the set of nodes having the most information propagation influence so as to propagate the information in the social network to finally maximize the information propagation range. Influence maximization is widely applied to important scenes of our daily life, such as marketing, advertisement, public opinion pre-warning, water quality monitoring, Internet campaign, and emergency notification.

In recent years, influence maximization has been emphasized by academic field and industry at home and abroad. Relevant researches and discussions have been published on international top conferences such as SIGKDD (ACM Conference on Knowledge Discovery and Data Mining), WWW (International Conference of World Wide Web), AAAI (Association for the Advancement of Artificial Intelligence), and ICDM (International Conference on Data Mining). At present, the academic field has had a deep study on the influence propagation model. The independent cascade model and liner threshold value model are widely studied. The current social network has large scale, specifically, the number of nodes is large, the association relation among nodes is complex, and the dynamic nature of the social network becomes stronger. These features bring great challenges for solving the influence maximization problem. The running time, algorithm precision, and extensibility are important factors that need to be considered when solving the influence maximization problem in the current large-scale social network environment. The existing two mainstream calculation methods for influence maximization, greedy algorithm and heuristic algorithm, can't meet requirements of short running time and high algorithm precision simultaneously. Many greedy algorithms for influence maximization are proposed, such as BasicGreedy, CELF, MixGreedy, and CELF++, and have high solution precision. But they have long running time, and can't be applied to the current social network that rapidly develops. Compared with the greedy algorithm, the proposed heuristic algorithms such as DegreeDiscount, PMIA, LDAG, and IRIE discover influential nodes quickly based on heuristic information, and significantly reduce the running time but still can't meet large-scale social network requirements. Moreover, the heuristic algorithm is far from the greedy algorithm in terms of precision so that the existing heuristic algorithm can't be applied to application scenes requiring high requirements on the running time and algorithm precision, such as marketing and water quality monitoring. Therefore, when the high precision is met, how to efficiently solve the influence maximization problem of the large-scale social network is an urgent and challenging study.

The study on the influence maximization of the social network can provide important economic benefits and social benefits. For example, for the social network-based word of mouth marketing and advertising, how to maximize brand promotion effects and propagation ranges by promoting commodities and advertisements to which users and propagating information and effects. For the water quality monitoring and epidemic monitoring, how to maximize the monitoring range and promptly discover water quality pollution and epidemic outbreaks by positioning which places for water quality monitoring and epidemic monitoring. In conclusion, the study on the influence maximization of the large-scale social network provides very important research and application values.

1.5 Organization of this book

This book starts from three scientific questions in online social network analysis, and then profoundly and systematically elaborates the fundamental theories, key methods and technologies of online social network analysis at three levels "structure and evolution–group and interaction–information and dissemination" by answering the three questions. Chapters of this book are arranged as shown in Figure 1.3.

1. "Structure and evolution"
Covering Chapters 2, 3, and 4.

Chapter 2 Social Network Structure Analysis and Modeling: it mainly introduces common network statistics characteristics of online social network analysis, summarizes and analyzes the general laws revealed from statistics characteristics of online social network, such as small-world phenomenon and power law distribution, and focuses on introducing the structure modeling methods for social network.

Chapter 3 Techniques and Approaches for Virtual Community Detection: it summaries the definition of the virtual community structure, divides the currently prevailing virtual community detection algorithms into static computation detection algorithms and dynamic computation detection algorithms, and introduces related research works in virtual community detection algorithms on this basis.

Chapter 4 Evolution Analysis of Virtual Communities: it analyzes evolution of virtual communities mainly from three aspects: formation mechanisms of virtual communities, influencing factors on the evolution of virtual communities, and detection algorithms of virtual communities.

2. "Group and interaction"
Covering Chapters 5, 6, 7, and 8.

Chapter 5 User Behavior Analysis: it introduces the influencing factors, modeling methods, and verification processes of social network adoption behavior and user loyalty research, the modeling methods of social network content creation behavior and content consumption behavior, as well as the analysis methods of

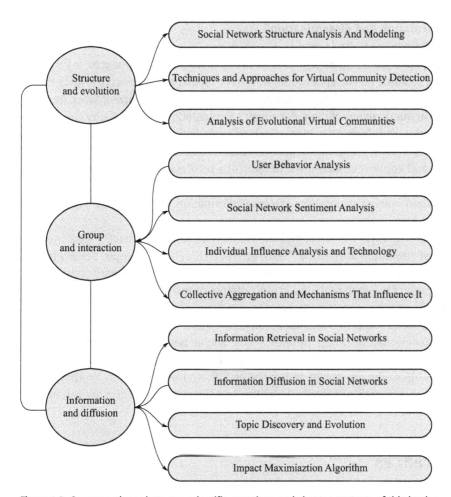

Figure 1.3: Correspondence between scientific questions and chapter contents of this book.

group interaction selection behavior, content selection behavior, and interaction time laws.

Chapter 6 Social Network Sentiment Analysis: it introduces sentiment analysis problems emerging in social networks by combining structure characteristics and group interaction characteristics of social networks.

Chapter 7 Individual Influence Analysis and Techniques: it correspondingly explains social network individual influence research from three aspects: social network influence strength calculation, individual influence calculation, and influence test.

Chapter 8 Collective Aggregation and the Mechanisms that Influence It: it discusses collective aggregation and the mechanisms that influence it based on collective intelligence and group polarization.

3. "Information and dissemination"

Covering Chapters 9, 10, 11, and 12.

Chapter 9 Information Retrieval in Social Networks: it introduces information retrieval research on social networks with three typical applications of search, classification, and recommendation, and mainly summarizes the current work on three aspects of query representation, document representation, and similarity calculation.

Chapter 10 Information Dissemination Laws in Social Networks: it elaborates network structure, group status, and information characteristic-based dissemination models and application examples, introduces a prediction method for dissemination statuses based on known information and its application examples, describes an information tracing method for tracking information dissemination sources, and analyzes some cases.

Chapter 11 Topic Discovery and Evolution: It introduces in detail a topic model— the most important theoretical basis in research related to topic discovery and evolution, separately introduces the related scientific research statuses of two urgent and important research problems in topic discovery and evolution of social networks, and analyzes their respective technical characteristics.

Chapter 12 Influence Maximization Calculation Method: The modeling basis of influence maximization problems is a social network graph and its corresponding influence dissemination model. It summarizes influence maximization problems in the social networks and their main research methods, and focuses on research of greedy algorithm and heuristic algorithm for calculating influence maximization.

References

[1]   Linton C. Freeman. The Development of Social Network Analysis: A Study in the Sociology of Science. Empirical Press, Vancouver, BC Canada, 2004.
[2]   Social Network[EB/OL]. Wikipedia [cited on March 12, 2014].
[3]   Lee Rainie, Barry Wellman. Networked: The New Social Operating System[M]. London: The MIT Press, 2012.
[4]   Ritzer, George; Goodman, Douglas. Sociological Theory (6/e)[M]. Taipei: McGraw-Hill, 2011: 32 and 33.
[5]   Gustave Le Bon (author), Dai Guangnian (translator). The Crowd (2nd Edition)[M]. Beijing: New World Press, 2011.
[6]   Georg Simmel. Sociology[EB/OL]. Wikipedia [cited on 28 February, 2014].
[7]   Jonathan H. Turner(author), Qiu Zeqi, Zhang maoyuan, et al. (translators). The Structure of Sociological Theory (7th Edition)[M]. Beijing: Huaxia Publishing House, 2006.
[8]   Barry Wellman, S. D Berkowitz. Social Structures: A Network Approach[M]. Cambridge University Press, 1988.
[9]   Zachary, W.W. An Information Flow Model for Conflict and Fission in Small Groups[J]. Journal of Anthropological Research, 1977, 33: 452–473.
[10]   Lewis Henry Morgan. The Indian Journals, 1859–1862[M]. New York: Dover Publications, 1993.

[11] A.R. Radcliffe-Brown (writer), Ding Guoyong (translator). Structure and Function In Primitive Society[M]. Beijing: China Social Sciences Press, 2009.

[12] Claude Lévi-Strauss (writer). The Elementary Structures of Kinship[M]. 1949.

[13] John List (writer), Liu Jun (translator). Social Network Analysis (2nd Edition)[M]. Chongqing: Chongqing University Press, 2007.

[14] Xia Xiyuan. Social Anthropology of Max Gluckman[D]. Beijing: Master's Thesis in Minzu University of China, 2010.

[15] Bruce Kapferer. Strategy and Transaction in an African Factory[M]. Manchester: Manchester University Press, 1972.

[16] Key Areas in the Public Sector Impact of Social Computing[EB/OL]. http//www.tno.nl/downloads/social_computing_impact_220609_final_report.pdf.

[17] Web2.0. Wikipedia [cited on 22 June, 2014].

[18] Victoria Shannon. A 'More Revolutionary' Web.: International Herald Tribune. 26 June, 2006.

[19] Web3.0. Wikipedia [cited on 07 December, 2013].

[20] A.R. Radcliffe-Brown. On Social Structure. The Journal of the Royal Anthropological Institute of Great Britain and Ireland, 1940, 70 (1): 1–12.

[21] Liu Hong. Influence of Social Communication on Mass Communication[EB/OL]. http://qnjz.dzwww.com/tyzg/201401/t20140107_9480720.htm.

[22] http://v.ifeng.com/news/tech/201108/f46b19ae-a683-43a1-a22c-9a1a8610d690.shtml.

[23] http://article.yeeyan.org/view/326883/280757.

[24] http://news.ynxxb.com/content/2011-8/21/N95832747960.as.

[25] https://alpha.app.net/hackernews/post/30997359.

[26] http://www.nature.com/srep/2013/130828/srep02522/full/srep02522.html.

[27] http://www.chinadaily.com.cn/hqzx/2012-08/25/content_15705243.htm.

[28] http://blog.csdn.net/smarttony/article/details/6839076.

[29] http://www.dmclick.com/daynews/detail.asp?id=1552.

[30] http://globalvoicesonline.org/specialcoverage/2011-special-coverage/egypt-protests-2011/.

[31] Watts D J, Strogatz S H. Collective Dynamics of 'Small-World' Networks[J]. Nature, 1998, 393 (6684): 440–442.

[32] Barabási A L, Albert R, Jeong H. Mean-Field Theory for Scale-Free Random Networks[J]. Physica A: Statistical Mechanics and its Applications, 1999, 272 (1): 173–187.

[33] http://zh.wikipedia.org/wiki/虚拟社群.

[34] Howard Rheingold (1993). The Virtual Community: Homesteading on the Electronic Frontier. London: MIT Press.

[35] Easley D, Kleinberg J. Networks, Crowds, and Markets: Reasoning about a Highly Connected World[M]. Cambridge University Press, 2010.

[36] Lazarsfeld P F, Katz E. Personal Influence: The Part Played by People in the Flow of Mass Communications[J]. Glencoe, Illinois, 1955.

[37] Arthur F. Bentley. Review of The Crowd by G. Le Bon[J]. American Journal of Sociology. 1897 (2): 612–614.

[38] Diggle T. Water: How Collective Intelligence Initiatives Can Address This Challenge[J]. Foresight, 2013, 15 (5): 342–353.

[39] Goedert J D, Sekpe V D. Decision Support System–Enhanced Scheduling in Matrix Organizations Using the Analytic Hierarchy Process[J]. Journal of Construction Engineering and Management, 2013, 139 (11).

[40] http://www.cnblogs.com/AndyJee/p/3480273.html.

[41] http://zh.wikipedia.org/zh-cn.

[42] http://wiki.mbalib.com/wiki/TDT.

Jin Xu and Hongli Zhang

2 Social network structure analysis and modeling

2.1 Introduction

Social network forms based on social communication relationship between individuals in a society. Individuals, as nodes in a network, are participants involved in social activities, which can be entities such as organizations and persons or virtual individuals such as network IDs. The relationship between individuals can be family relations, behavior interactions, sending and receiving messages, and many others. The interactions between individuals include establishing or releasing acquaintance relationship and participating in the same topic discussion. These diverse individual behaviors in social network promote continuous evolution of network structure, which characterize social network with user group interaction and information dissemination and evolution.

With respect to social network structure analysis, many studies have illustrated that a variety of real-world social networks have common structural characteristics of complex networks such as small-world phenomenon, scale-free law, and power-law distribution. With respect to social network structure modeling, many scholars have tried to conduct quantitative analysis on social networks using graph model. Many breakthroughs have been achieved in recent years, such as small-world model in which randomness is introduced into the regular network through reconnection mechanism, as well as scale-free model featured by power-law distribution as a result of "preferential attachment" rule between nodes. Overall, the understanding of social network structure can be divided into the following three stages: First, as there are usually tens of millions of nodes and even more edges in social network, it is impossible to plot the real network structure. Usually, statistical characteristics of network are needed, i.e., when facing a large number of social network instances in real-world, we should obtain a preliminary description of the network structure by corresponding network parameters. Second, collecting and analyzing the static and evolution characteristics of certain network parameters in a large number of network instances to determine the general laws of social network. Finally, establishing corresponding network models to express these laws to understand the intrinsic mechanism in generating these laws.

This chapter is organized as follows: Section 2.2 first shows an example of a small online social network to facilitate the description and discussion. Following the three step-by-step stages introduced above, Section 2.3 mainly introduces the common characteristics of online social network and defines them giving corresponding formal descriptions. Based on Section 2.3, Section 2.4 summarizes and analyzes

https://doi.org/10.1515/9783110599374-002

general laws from statistical characteristics of online social network, such as small-world phenomenon, and power-law distribution. By introducing some important network structure models in complex network research and corresponding instances generated, Section 2.5 introduces the structure modeling methods for social network, including WS and its extension models, BA and its extension models, as well as other models available for social network modeling, such as forest-fire model, Kronecker graph model, and production model.

2.2 Examples

In social networks, many individuals participate in activities and the structure of network is complex. Using graph theory, a mathematical tool, social network can be intuitively described as a graph. Let $G = \{V,E\}$ denotes the social network, where V denotes a node set with each node representing a person and E denotes an edge set, and each directed or undirected edge set denoting the relationship between two persons. Figure 2.1 illustrates a typical structure of online social network with some nodes and edges in Sina Weibo.

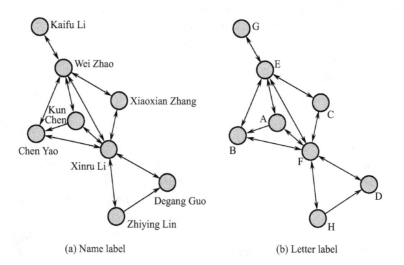

(a) Name label   (b) Letter label

Figure 2.1: Social graph in Sina Weibo.

In Figure 2.1, we select eight users from the top ten (ranked by the number of followers) from Sina Weibo to form a typical user following relationship network. We obtain many interesting conclusions by some simple analyses on Figure 2.1, such as these eight persons have different backgrounds divided into five classes: ① "Famous Big V" (public intellectual) in scientific and academic circles and industrial circles Kaifu Li; ② Movie and TV stars Wei Zhao, Chen Yao, Kun Chen, Xinru Lin; ③Famous writer Xiaoxian Zhang; ④ Actor, singer, racing driver Zhiying Lin;⑤ Crosstalk master Degang Guo. Its obvious that there are following relationships between four movie and TV stars, forming a tight social circle. Zhiying Lin and Xinru Lin from China TaiWan only follow each other. In Figure 2.1, Wei Zhao and Xinru Lin have the largest number of fans, and establish relationships with persons from different classes by following each other, which makes them the bridge linking persons in different area. Zhiying Lin and Degang Guo, Kun Chen, and Chen Yao have unidirectional following relationship. These data were collected on 22:00, 06 April 2014.

By changing names in Figure 2.1(a) into letters, as shown in Table 2.1 for convenience, we obtain Figure 2.1(b).

Table 2.1: Comparison table for names and letters.

Name label	Kun Chen	Chen Yao	Xiaoxian Zhang	Degang Guo	Wei Zhao	Xinru Lin	Kaifu Li	Zhiying Lin
Letter label	A	B	C	D	E	F	G	H

2.3 Statistical characteristics of social network

In many mathematical subjects, statistics is an important tool to describe uncertainty problems. In the context of big data, analyzing and mining large and various data demand the support of statistical knowledge. Because data in social networks has typical characteristics of big data and often contains some noisy data, statistical methods are needed for its description. In this section, we will introduce some elementary statistical characteristics of social network, including degree distribution, average path length, and clustering coefficient, which will be the foundation of following sections.

2.3.1 Degree distribution

Degree is an important characteristic to describe the nature of node, which is defined as the number of edges connected to the node. In directed networks, degree is divided into out-degree and in-degree. For a node, the out-degree is the number of edges from it to other nodes and the in-degree is the number of edges from other nodes to it. The average degree of a network $\langle k \rangle$ is the average degree of all the nodes in the network, which reflects the density of network and degree distribution is used to describe the importance of different nodes according to their distribution law of degree. By calculating the degree of each node and ranking nodes according to their serial numbers, we obtain the degree sequence of the network based on which the degree distribution is obtained by calculating the frequency of node degree. It is worth noting that, though we lose the one-to-one correspondence between each node and its degree when calculating the degree distribution according to degree sequence, degree distribution can fully describe the law of degree distribution and identify the different types of networks when the network scale is big. For example, ER random graph follows Poisson distribution and complex networks such as online social network follow power-law distribution.

Degree distribution of nodes in networks can be described as follows:
(1) Function of degree distribution $P(k)$. $P(k)$ indicates the percentage of nodes with the degree of k in the network.
(2) Function of cumulative degree distribution P_k. P_k indicates the probability distribution of nodes with degree no less than k, and its distribution relationship is:

$$P_k = \sum_{x-k}^{\infty} P(x) \tag{2.1}$$

We call the network as a scale-free network following power-law distribution if its node degree follows distribution function $P(k) \propto k^{-\gamma}$ with power exponent of γ. The cumulative degree distribution function P_k of the network follows power distribution $P_k \propto k^{-(\gamma-1)}$ with power exponent of $\gamma-1$.

We can obtain the node degree in the network by analyzing the letter labeling network in Figure 2.1(b), with degree sequence shown in Table 2.2. We can further obtain node degree distribution shown in Table 2.3 by counting degree sequence.

Table 2.2: Degree sequence of nodes in networks shown in Figure 2.1(b).

Node	A	B	C	D	E	F	G	H
Degree	3	3	2	2	5	6	1	2

Table 2.3: Degree distribution of nodes in networks shown in Figure 2.1(b).

k	1	2	3	4	5	6	Total
P(k)	0.125	0.375	0.25	0	0.125	0.125	1

2.3.2 Average path length

The distance d_{ij} between any two users i and j in a social network is defined as the length of the path with the least edges between the users, also termed as the shortest path length. As shown in Figure 2.1(b), for all the nonrepeated paths between user G and user B, only G-E-B passes two edges, and the remaining passes more than two edges, making the shortest path length between G and B is G-E-B with a length of 2.

Average path length L is defined as the average length of the shortest path between any two nodes in the network; it is also termed as the average length of the network or characteristic path length of the network. It describes the cost of information transfer between nodes in the network. In online social networks, L is always used to measure the relationship between users, and represents the number of friends in the shortest path between any two users. It is calculated as follows:

$$L = \frac{2}{N(N-1)} \sum_{i=1}^{N} \sum_{j=i+1}^{N} d_{ij} \tag{2.2}$$

where N denotes the number of nodes in the network, and d_{ij} denotes the shortest path length between nodes i and j.

Diameter D is defined as the maximum of all the shortest path lengths, i.e.,

$$D = \max_{1 \le i,j \le N} d_{ij} \tag{2.3}$$

Effective diameter is often used instead of diameter in social networks. The reason is that real social networks usually are not always fully connected as it includes many discrete nodes and connected branches. This issue can be avoided effectively when we select 90% of the nodes, i.e., the minimum value which is larger than distances between at least 90% interconnected node pairs is called effective diameter [15]. The network diameter in Figure 2.1(b) is 3, with the corresponding shortest path being G-E-F-H or G-E-F-D.

Example 2.1 Calculate the average path length and diameter of the network shown in Figure 2.1(b).

Solution: First, calculate the distances between all node pairs: $d_{GE} = 1$; $d_{GB} = 2$; $d_{GA} = 2$; $d_{GC} = 2$; $d_{GF} = 2$; $d_{GH} = 3$; $d_{GD} = 3$; $d_{EB} = 1$; $d_{EA} = 1$; $d_{EC} = 1$; $d_{EF} = 1$; $d_{EH} = 2$; $d_{ED} = 2$; $d_{BA} = 1$; $d_{BE} = 1$; $d_{BC} = 2$; $d_{BH} = 2$; $d_{BD} = 2$; $d_{AF} = 1$; $d_{AC} = 2$; $d_{AD} = 2$; $d_{AH} = 2$; $d_{CF} = 1$; $d_{CH} = 2$; $d_{CD} = 2$; $d_{FH} = 1$; $d_{ED} = 1$; $d_{DH} = 1$.

Then, substitute the data above into Formula 2.2 to calculate average path length

$$L = \frac{2}{8 \times (8-1)} \sum_{i \ne j} d_{ij} = 1.64$$

According to Formula 2.3, we obtain the diameter as $D = \max_{1 \le i,j \le N} d_{ij} = d_{GH} = d_{GD} = 3$

2.3.3 Density

Density $d(G)$ describes the dense degree of interconnections between nodes in a network. It is the ratio between the actual and the maximal number of edges in the network, and is used to measure the dense degree and evolution trend of social relations in online social networks [15]. The density of a network with N node(s) and L actual edge(s) is expressed as follows:

$$d(G) = \frac{2L}{N(N-1)} \tag{2.4}$$

The range of density is [0,1]. When the network is fully connected, $d(G) = 1$. When there is no connected edge in the network, $d(G) = 0$. There is nearly no network with density of 1, and the maximal density found in real network is 0.5 [1]. In addition, the density of large-scale network is generally smaller than that of the small-scale network. Densities of networks with different scale cannot be compared directly but can be compared by absolute density formula [2].

$$d(G) = M/[4SR^3/3D] \tag{2.5}$$

where D denotes the diameter, R denotes radius, and S denotes perimeter calculated according to diameter.

In the network of Figure 2.1(b), we obtain density $d(G) = \frac{24}{8 \times (8-1)} = 0.43$ by substituting the number of nodes $N = 8$ and real number of connected edges $L = 12$ into Formula 2.4.

2.3.4 Clustering coefficient

Clustering coefficient is used to describe the degree that nodes connected to the same node in a network are also adjacent nodes. For a node v_i, its clustering coefficient C_i describes the average probability that it connects to adjacent nodes. k_i denotes the number of neighbors connected to v_i and e_i denotes the actual undirected edges existing among k_i neighbors. It is easy to know that $\frac{k_i(k_i-1)}{2}$ is the maximum of links among these k_i neighbors, thus clustering coefficient of node v_i can be described as follows:

$$C_i = \frac{2e_i}{k_i(k_i-1)} \tag{2.6}$$

Clustering coefficient of a node has intuitive meaning in social networks. Informally, it is the probability that friends of the same person are also friends, and reflects the closeness of acquaintance among a person's friends in his/her circle of friends. As most persons in one's circle of friends are their classmates, colleagues, and relatives, its highly possible that they know each other. Thus, social networks have strong aggregation. Average clustering coefficient is used to describe network aggregation.

Average clustering coefficient is the average of clustering coefficient of all nodes in a network, and the formula is as follows:

$$C = \frac{1}{|V|} \sum_{i \in V} C_i \tag{2.7}$$

where $|V|$ denotes the number of nodes in the network; C_i denotes the clustering coefficient of v_i with range of value as $[0,1]$; $C = 0$ indicates that there is no edge in the network; and $C = 1$ indicates that the network is fully connected.

The average clustering coefficient describes the probability that each of the two users of any three users know each other, which reflects the closeness of acquaintance among users in the network.

Example 2.2 Calculate clustering coefficient of every node in and the average clustering coefficient of the network shown in Figure 2.1(b).

Solution: In Figure 2.1(b), nodes B, E, and F directly connect to node A, the maximal number of probable edges among the three nodes is $3 \times (3 - 2) = 3$, and there are three edges, thus the clustering coefficient of node A is $C_A = 3/3 = 1$ according to Formula 2.6. Similarly, the clustering coefficients of other nodes are shown in Table 2.4.

According to the clustering coefficient of each node shown in Table 2.4, we obtain the clustering coefficient of the network shown in Figure 2.1(b) by Formula 2.7.

Table 2.4: Clustering coefficient distribution of nodes in the network shown in Figure 2.1(b).

Node	B	C	D	E	F	G	H
C_i	1	1	1	$1/6$	$1/6$	0	1

2.3.5 Betweenness

Betweenness describes the capacity of nodes to be part of the shortest paths in the network. Betweenness of a node (or an edge) is the sum of probabilities that shortest paths go through the node (or the edge), reflecting the impact and centrality of a node in a network. Assuming that the number of the shortest paths between nodes i and j is δ_{ij}, and the number of the shortest paths going through a node k is $\delta_{ij}(k)$, then the ratio $\delta_{ij}(k)/\delta_{ij}$ can describe the importance of node k between i and j. Based on this, the betweenness of node k is defined as follows:

$$C_B(k) = \sum_{i \in V} \sum_{j \neq i \in V} \frac{\delta_{ij}(k)}{\delta_{ij}} \tag{2.8}$$

Betweenness is used to evaluate the capacity of traffic overhead in the internet. Bigger betweenness C_B of a node indicates that more information can go through it during information dissemination. Some hub nodes used for data transmission usually has high usage rate with bigger data volume, which causes network congestion. In social networks, degree is used to measure the importance of a node. Although the degrees of nodes connecting different communities may be small, they are extremely important; thus their betweennesses are usually relatively big. Hence, betweenness is used to evaluate the importance of a user in the information transmission between all user pairs in social networks.

Example 2.3 Calculate betweenness of each node in the network shown in Figure 2.1(b).

Solution: According to the definition of betweenness, in the example shown in Figure 2.1(b), only nodes F and E are on the shortest paths between other node pairs in the entire network. The number of shortest paths going through node F is 10, i.e., A-F-D, B-F-D, E-F-D, C-F-D, G-F-D, A-F-H, B-F-H, E-F-H, C-F-H, and G-F-H. In addition, there are two shortest paths (from node B to C and from node A to C) going through node E or F, so we obtain $C_B(F) = 8 + 1/2 + 1/2 = 9$ by Formula 2.8. The shortest paths going through E are H-E-B, H-E-C, H-E-A, H-E-F, H-E-G, H-E-D, B-E-C, and A-E-C, hence, the betweenness of node E is $C_B(F) = 6 + 1/2 + 1/2 = 7$. The betweennesses of all nodes are shown in Table 2.5.

Table 2.5: Betweenness distribution in the network shown in Figure 2.1(b).

Node	A	B	C	D	E	F	G	H
C_B	0	0	0	0	7	9	0	0

2.4 Social networking characteristics analysis

This section describes and analyzes the regularities represented by the statistic characteristic in the social network. We focus on two important statistic characteristic in the topological research on social network: small-world phenomenon and scale-free characteristic. Small-world phenomenon indicates that the distance among individuals in the social network are very short, which is proved by calculating the average path length in the network. Scale-free characteristic indicates that the node degree in the social network follows power-law distribution. Subsequently, this section introduces assortativity and reciprocity of the social network. In addition, we introduce several typical online social networks, and analyze the performance of these characteristics in different online social networks.

2.4.1 Small-world phenomenon

Two people with long geographical distance tend to have shorter social relation interval. Sometimes people may find that someone who seems "distant" is actually "very close" to you. In 1929, the Hungarian author Frigyes Karinthy proposed six degrees of segmentation for the first time in his short story "The Chain." He stated that, although there are great physical distances between individuals around the world, the increasingly stronger human relations make the actual social distance between each other much more smaller. Two strangers can establish connection through five persons at most. In 1967, Stanley Milgram, a social psychology professor at Harvard University, summarized and proposed the famous "Six Degrees of Separation Hypothesis" by designing a letter delivery experiment [5]. Milgram randomly chose 296 volunteers in Omaha, Nebraska as the initial sender to mail the letter and asked them to give this letter to a stockbroker in Boston. In their experience, each person made contact alone. Milgram told each sender the recipient's information, including name, location, occupation, and if they did not know the recipient, they send the letter to an acquaintance that may know the recipient. In this manner, the chain of the sender forms, and each member of the chain was trying to send this letter to their friends, family members, colleagues, or acquaintances to transfer letters to their recipient as soon as possible. Professor Milgram found that 60 chains eventually reached the recipient, with an average of six steps. Milgram made the following conclusion: any two persons can remain in touch through an average of five acquaintances within six steps. The study unprecedentedly proved that human society is a small-world network with a shorter path length characteristic. Like the classic lines in John Guare's movie "Six Degrees of Segmentation" shot after more than 20 years: "I am able to obtain in touch the President of the United States or a boatman in Venice as long as the right five persons between us are found."

Small-world phenomenon was further confirmed by two famous real experiments [39], i.e., interesting Kevin Bacon game and Erdös number. In 1997, three American students invented the Kevin Bacon game. They considered Kevin Bacon, a movie actor, as the center of the filmdom. In Kevin Bacon game, if a movie costars a person and Kevin Bacon, his/her Bacon number is 1. The majority of actors/actresses in the world can build a direct or indirect acquaintance relationship with Bacon within six steps, i.e., the Bacon number of less than or equal to 6. For example, the Bacon number of Ziyi Zhang, a famous actress in China, is 2 as she and Laurence Fishburne both participated in the dubbing of the animation movie of "Teenage Mutant Ninja Turtles", and Laurence Fishburne cooperates with Kevin Bacon in "Mystic River."

In fact, after analyzing more than 1.7 million actors/actresses, only 260 people's Bacon number is greater than 6, and the average Bacon number of all actors/actresses is 3. Paul Erdös, a famous mathematician, has proposed the random graph theory. Erdös numbers among mathematicians is: Erdös marked himself as 0, people who had directly worked with Erdös marked as 1, and persons were marked as 2 if they directly worked with the persons with Erdös number of 1. If a person has multiple Erdös numbers, the smallest shall be chosen and so on. However, no matter how far the distance of industry and directions between other mathematicians and Erdös, their Erdös numbers are extremely small. For example, Einstein's Erdös number is 2, Fermi's Erdös number is 3, Pauli's Erdös number is 4, and Heisenberg's Erdös number is 4. Erdös number of Bill Gates who only published one article on information theory is 4. In addition, social networks tend to show high clustering characteristics. For example, students of the same major in the school may know each other, and student of the same class may be friends. "Triple Transfer Ratio," a popular concept in sociology, describes a common phenomenon that a person's friends may also be friends.

Therefore, networks with social relationship tend to have relatively large aggregation, just like Milgram's experiment on small-world phenomenon. In 1998, two young physicists, Duncan Watts and Steven Strogatz [24], published a landmark article in "Nature" where they proposed the concept of small-world network and set up a small-world model.

Take Figure 2.1(a) as an example, most shortest path lengths between stars are 1 or 2. The largest length of the shortest path is Degang Guo and Kaifu Li, with distance in Sina Weibo of $d\,(G, D) = 3$. According to Example 2.1 listed in the length of the shortest path between all nodes, we can obtain the shortest path length distribution of the network in Figure 2.1(b) are shown in Table 2.6 below. $P(d)$ denotes the probability that the shortest path length is d:

$$L = \sum_{0 < i < N} dP(d) = 1 \times \frac{3}{7} + 2 \times \frac{1}{2} + 3 \times \frac{1}{14} = 1.64$$

Table 2.6: Distribution of star network in Sina Weibo.

Shortest path length d	1	2	3
$P(d)$	3/7	1/2	1/14

We can see that the distance between any two stars in the star network in Sina Weibo is less than 2.

As the extension of the social network, the online social network also features significant small-world phenomenon. Shorter average path length of the network results in more evident small-world phenomenon. Compared with traditional complex networks, the online social network has shorter average path length and effective diameter, with its effective diameter being far less than the Web [3] and its average path length only one-third of the Web. Ahn et al. [4, 23] studied the average path length distribution of the Cyworld, an online social network. We used the entire network topology in December 2005 of Cyworld, the biggest social network site for making friends in South Korea, as our dataset provided by operators, which is a complete dataset containing 12 million user nodes and 190 million edges composed of friendly relationship. The measurement of the average path length of the network is divided into two steps. first, sample different number of seeds to randomly obtain 100, 2000, and 3000 nodes, and then compare their data with the original data containing all nodes. Second, use BFS to

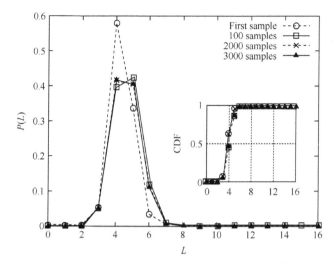

Figure 2.2: The distribution situation of the average path length of the Cyworld, an online social network in South Korea [4].

obtain the average path length of users, as shown in Figure 2.2. We can see that the average path length of sampling network converges to the average path length of the entire network, and the shortest path length between most nodes is 4~5, whereas the average path length between the seed node and more than 90% nodes is less than 6. When measuring the average path length of the large-scale user graph, sampling is usually used to reduce the time for BFS. Jure Leskovec and Eric Horvitz [38] screened the Microsoft MSN chatting records in 2006, and analyzed 30 billion pieces communication information of 240 million active users. As the data was too large, they random chose 1000 users by sampling and calculated the average path length of the network. They found that 48% of the users can be associated within six steps, and the average path length of the MSN network is only 6.6.

There are some differences between the average path length of different types of online social networks [3, 4]. Networks mainly used for sharing have larger length than those mainly used for making friends. Online social networks that are mainly for making friends usually have a smaller average path length and closer social ties, as well as more significant small-world phenomenon. With the development of online social networks, online world seems to be closer than the "Six Degrees of Separation," as the online social network further narrows the distance between persons. In 2011, the data team of Facebook counted the entire network dataset (approximately 720 million user nodes, 69 billion connected edges of friend relationship) found that the average path length between any two users is only 4.74 [6]. In online social networks such as microblog, users can establish connected edge by following other users. According to the research of Sysomos, a social media monitoring company, on 5.2 billion similar connected edge relationship, the average path length of Twitter is 4.67. On average, approximately 50% persons are only four steps away on Twitter, and any individuals from two networks may be associated within five steps.

2.4.2 Scale-free characteristic

In nature and social life, events interesting scientists often have a typical scale, and changes of individual scale in the vicinity of the characteristic scale are very small. For example, a person's height distribution, the number of passengers waiting in the bus stand and so on follows Poisson distribution. As shown in the Figure 2.3(c), most individual data concentrate in the vicinity of the average degree of the network $\langle k \rangle$ and tend to node with the number of individuals far away from the average value decreasing exponentially; thus, we call $\langle k \rangle$ as the characteristic scale of network with homogeneity. Degree distribution of some real networks is quite different, such as the degree distribution of wealth, national population, and number of friends on the dating site. Individuals are quite different from each other in data systems of such real networks. Most nodes have a small amount of connected edges while few nodes have a large number of connected edges. The network present heterogeneity due to the lack of a unified measurement scale, and for those characteristic scales without limited measurement distribution range in node degree distribution, we call this feature scale-free. In the random network, as shown in Figure 2.3(a), the average node degree is approximately 2. However, scale-free network, as shown in Figure 2.3 (b), some red nodes have high degrees, and connects to many nodes in the network, while the remaining nodes have small degrees. In 1999, American physicist Albert-Laszlo Barabasi and his student Reka Albert [7] found that the degree distribution of such heterogeneous networks follows power-law distribution: $P(k) \propto k^{-\gamma}$ with power-law exponent being γ. They call this form of distribution network as scale-free network and the power-law distribution degree of degree of network node as scale-free characteristic.

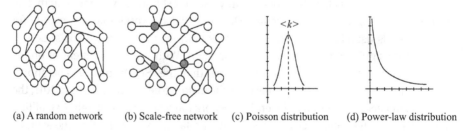

(a) A random network   (b) Scale-free network   (c) Poisson distribution   (d) Power-law distribution

Figure 2.3: Random networks and scale-free networks and their distribution characteristics.

Heavy-tailed phenomenon is an important characteristic of power-law distribution in scale-free networks. As shown in Figure 2.3(d), power-law distribution does not have node value as Poisson distribution and drags a long tail curve. In general, degree distribution in online social networks have heavy-tailed phenomenon. Unlike Poisson distribution, probability $P(k)$ that a node with degree of k appears in power-law distribution does not decrease at an exponential rate while k increases; however, it gently and progressively tends to become 0, which shows the "long tail" nature. Long-tailed distribution is a subclass of heavy-tailed distribution, which was first pointed out by the Pareto Principle and Zipf's Law. In 1897, Italian economist Vilfredo Pareto studied the wealth and income patterns of the British in the 19th century, and found that the incomes of few persons are far more than that of other persons, promoting the famous "80/20 Rule," that is, 20% of the population accounted for 80% of the social wealth. In 1932, George Kingsley Zipf, a linguistics expert from Harvard University, studied the usage frequency of English words, and found that the usage frequencies of words are not uniform when arranging the words in descending order, but they follow the simple inverse relation with the power function as per its ranking, suggesting that only a handful of English words are often used while the vast majority of words are rarely used. In many real networks, the nodes with high degrees are rare compared with total number of nodes, but they played a "leading" role. Furthermore, these degree nodes give the network the nature completely different from uniform random network.

Random network model [8] assumes that the probability that any pair of nodes is interconnected is equal and its degree distribution $P(k)$ follows Poisson distribution. When node degree k tends to infinity, the speed that Poisson distribution $P(k)$ tends to 0 is between normal distribution e^{-k^2} and exponential distribution e^{-k}. While the speed that exponential distribution e^{-k} tends to speed 0 is already fast, the speed that Poisson distribution tends to speed 0 is much faster. However, overall, these three distributions are "narrow tail" or almost "no tail." We define the heavy-tailed phenomenon as follows, if the random variable X satisfies:

$$\lim_{x \to \infty} \frac{P(X > x)}{e^{-\lambda x}} = \infty \tag{2.9}$$

Then X have heavy tails. where λ is a positive integer. Heavy-tailed phenomenon implies that, when tends to positive infinity, the probability for X taking $X > x$ is low order infinitesimal following exponential distribution, which indicates a higher probabitlity than that of exponential distribution when the variable value is large. Obviously, for exponential distribution $p(x) = \lambda e^{-\lambda x}, x > 0$, substituted it into Formula 2.9 for verification:

$$\lim_{x \to \infty} \frac{P(X > x)}{e^{-\lambda x}} = \lim_{x \to \infty} \frac{e^{-\lambda x}}{e^{-\lambda x}} = 1 \neq \infty$$

Therefore, the exponential distribution does not have heavy tails [9].

According to mathematical analysis, it is easy to know that the variable X following power-law distribution $P(x) = cx^{-\gamma}$ has heavy tails. In addition, a class of distribution frequently appears in real networks, and has heavy tails. Power-law distribution truncated exponential, i.e., the variable X follow the distribution of $P(x) \propto x^{-\gamma}e^{-\lambda x}$.

After publishing a landmark article in Nature and proposed the scale-free network model, Albert-Laszlo Barabasi and Reka Albert [7] analyzed the degree distribution law of many real complex networks, such as the movie actor/actress collaboration network, World Wide Web, power grid of western United States, etc. The authors found that all these work similarly or exactly follow power-law distribution $P(k) \propto k^{-\gamma}$, and the power-law distribution exponent met $2 < \gamma < 3$, in which γ is a positive number. Their work reveals that important nodes (nodes with big degrees) in the actual networks distributed nonuniformly, but orderly. Figure 2.4(a) indicates the degree distribution of the actor/actress cooperation network, in which the nodes denote the actors/actresses and the edges denote the cooperation relationship between the actors/actresses. The number of nodes in the network is 212,250 with an average degree of 28.78. Take logarithm for two sides of equation as $P(k) = ak^{-\gamma}$ and obtain $\log P(k) = \log a - \gamma \log k$, i.e., if a power-law relationship exists, the function taking $\log k$ as the variable will be a straight line with a slope of $-\gamma$ in double logarithmic coordinate. Degree distribution network of actor/actress cooperation presents a power-law distribution $P(k) \propto k^{-\gamma_{actor}}$ with the exponent as $\gamma_{actor} = 2.3 \pm 0.1$. In the World Wide Web, nodes are web pages and edges are hyperlink relationships between webpages. As shown in Figure 2.4 (b), the dataset is a subset of the World Wide Web containing 325,729 nodes and follow power-law distribution $P(k) \propto k^{-\gamma_{www}}$ with the exponent as $\gamma_{www} = 2.1 \pm 0.1$. In electricity network, nodes are motors, transformers, or substations and edges are the transmission lines between them. As shown in Figure 2.4(c), the power grid of western United States has 4,941 nodes, and its degree distribution follows power-law distribution $\gamma_{power} = 4$.

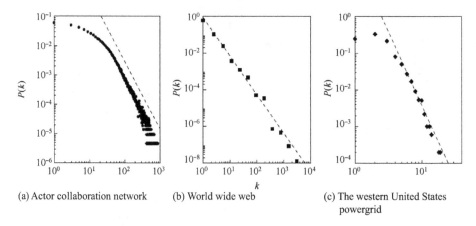

(a) Actor collaboration network (b) World wide web (c) The western United States powergrid

Figure 2.4: Diagram of network degree distribution [7].

Many actual measurement studies on online social network show that social networks have scale-free characteristic. Most users have relatively few social relations whereas some users have more social relations, and the degree of distribution follows power-law distribution. Mislove et al. [3] studied topological characteristics of the largest connected subgraphs of four online social networks (Flickr, LiveJournal, YouTube, and Orkut). Flickr is a photo sharing website with an important characteristic of the extension of personal relationships and content organization based on social network. LiveJournal is an online community providing comprehensive social services including diary, blog, forum, dating. YouTube is a website mainly for video sharing where users can share videos on the website and download movies or short films and can even form a network community through friendships. Orkut, launched by Google, is an online community mainly for making friends. Orkut users can leave their personal or professional information to create a relationship between friends or join the virtual community due to the same interest.

There are statistical results of four kinds of online social network in Table 2.7. Registered users are defined as nodes, and each user's friend lists are defined as the edge from the node to other nodes, making the entire network graph a directed graph. These four kinds of online social networks impose no restrictions on customer relationship. Flickr, LiveJournal, and YouTube provide developers with open APIs to retrieve structured data, whereas social relationships in Orkut may be obtained only through web capturing. In addition, Orkut also limits the data scale that may be captured when accessing user account and login IP, making its data capturing scale smaller than the remaining three social networks. Figure 2.5 shows the CCDF graph of the four kinds of online social networks. It is easy to see that the degree distribution of the distributed online social networks follow power-law distribution. In out-degree distribution of Orkut and LiveJournal, inflection point appears due to their limit on the number of friends in each node. In addition to the limit on the number of friends, data capturing method of BFS algorithm make the samples from nodes with low degree too few, resulting in possible measurement bias in the degree distribution on Orkut.

Table 2.7: Statistical results of 4 kinds of online social networks.

	Flickr	LiveJournal	Orkut	YouTube
Nodes	1,846,198	5,284,457	3,072,441	11,578,872
Capturing percentage	26.9%	95.4%	11.3%	Unknown
Number of edges	22,613,981	77,402,652	223,534,301	4,945,382
Average node degree	12.24	16.97	106.1	4.29

We use maximum likelihood method [10] to fit curves in Figure 2.5 and the results are shown in Table 2.8, where Δ denotes fitting bias. Overall, there is a big difference between the exponents of out-degree and in-degree power-law distribution of Web, while the exponents of out-degree and in-degree power-law distribution of online

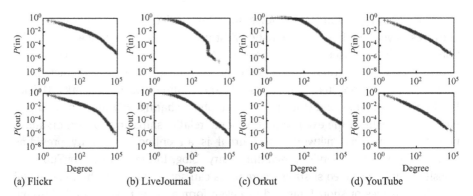

(a) Flickr (b) LiveJournal (c) Orkut (d) YouTube

Figure 2.5: CCDF graph of accumulative degree distribution of 4 kinds of online social network [3].

Table 2.8: Power-law exponent and bias of the degree distribution of several online social networks and Web [3].

Online social network	Out-degree		In-degree	
	T	Δ	T	Δ
Web	2.67	—	2.09	—
Flickr	1.74	0.057 5	1.78	0.027 8
LiveJournal	1.59	0.078 3	1.65	0.103 7
Orkut	1.50	0.631 9	1.50	0.6203
YouTube	1.63	0.131 4	1.99	—

social networks are similar and less than that of the Web as most friend relations in online social networks are bidirectional. Degree distribution of some online social networks is not monotonous power-law distribution. For example, Kwak et al. [11] found that in Twitter an online social network such as microblog, in class online, some users have a large number of "fans," and the distribution of "fans" does not follow power-law distribution. In addition, Twitter, as an online social network for resource and information sharing, has a number of star nodes that has a lot of fans.

In scale-free networks, nodes with a larger degree usually have smaller clustering coefficients, while nodes within smaller degree have larger clustering coefficients. In many real networks, the relation of clustering coefficient and degree follows power-law: $C(k) \propto k^{-\alpha}$, where $C(k)$ is the average clustering coefficient of nodes with degree of k and α is "level exponent," then the network hierarchy exists [12], i.e., the network can be clearly classified into several distinctive levels. Erzsebet Ravasz and Albert-Laszlo Barabasi found that scale-free networks have different hierarchies with close connection inside the group, however, the average degree of nodes is small with sparse connection inside the group while hub nodes responsible for connections have relatively big degree. They also pointed out that the average clustering coefficients of networks such as actor/actress cooperation network and the internet substantially accords with decreasing power-law relationship.

Previous studies have shown that the clustering coefficient distribution of many online social networks follow power-law distribution [13, 14] with a hierarchical structure. As shown in Figure 2.6, Cyworld [4], an online social network in South Korea, has an average clustering coefficient of 0.16, slightly less than other online social networks [3, 13], indicating that the relations between friends in Cyworld are relatively sparse. In addition, the clustering coefficient distribution also has obvious segment characteristics. The clustering coefficient meets the power-law distribution with exponent of 0.4 when $k < 500$ and sharply decline when $k > 500$, i.e., connections between the neighbors of nodes with degree value more than 500 are considerably sparser that that of those nodes with low degree. In general, nodes with small degrees in social networks have relatively high clustering coefficients and follow power-law distribution with some degree of hierarchy and relatively high aggregation, whereas nodes within the larger lower degree have low clustering coefficients and sparser distribution.

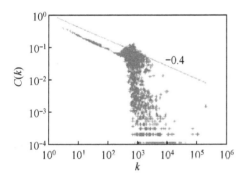

Figure 2.6: Clustering coefficient distribution of Cyworld [4].

2.4.3 Assortativity

Assortativity reflects the correlation degree among nodes with similar degrees in the network. Among them, the degree correlation indicates the correlation between the degree of a node and its neighbor nodes. In a network, if a node with larger (smaller) degree tends to connect a node with a larger (smaller) degree, the network has positive correlation, i.e., assortativity, otherwise the network has negative correlation, i.e., disassortativity. In general, we use two methods to measure the assortativity of the network: one is to draw a neighbor's average degree distribution and calculate the slope, and the other is to calculate assortativity coefficient of the network.

1. Distribution of Average Neighbor Degree
Usually, the distribution of average neighbor degree is calculated through degree correlation function k_{nn}, which is defined as the average value of neighbor degree of a node with degree of k, and the calculation formula is:

$$k_{nn}(k) = \sum_{k'}(k'P(k'|k)) \qquad (2.10)$$

where conditional probability $P(k'|k)$ is the probability that there are edges between nodes with degree of k and k'. In fact, when calculating k_{nn}, we usually choose average neighbor degree of one node to replace it. First, average neighbor degree of node v_i is defined as:

$$k_{nn,i} = \frac{1}{k_i}\sum_j a_{ij}k_j \qquad (2.11)$$

where k_i denotes the degree of node v_i, a_{ij} is an adjacent matrix element. If v_i and v_j are connected, $a_{ij} = 1$, or $a_{ij} = 0$. So, the average value $k_{nn}(k)$ of average neighbor degree of all nodes with degree of k is defined as:

$$k_{nn}(k) = \frac{1}{|M_k|}\sum_{i\in M_k} k_{nn,i} \qquad (2.12)$$

where M_k denotes the set of nodes with degree of k, $|M_k|$ is the node number of the set. In scale-free network, nodes with larger degree are minority, so a node with larger degree has smaller average neighbor degree. If $k_{nn}(k)$ is an increasing function with increasing k, then it indicates that nodes with larger degree tends to connect with each other and such network is assortative network, otherwise it is disassortative network.

Example 2.4 Calculate the distribution of average neighbor degree of the following network in Figure 2.1 (b), and determine the network type.

Solution: Substitute degree sequence of each node listed in Table 2.2 into Formula (2.11) to calculate the average neighbor degree of nodes:
k_{nn}, $G = \deg(E) = 5$, k_{nn}, $C = [\deg(E) + \deg(F)]/2 = 11/2$. In a similar manner, we can calculate average neighbor degree of other nodes:
k_{nn}, $E = 14/5$, k_{nn}, $B = 14/3$, k_{nn}, $A = 14/3$, k_{nn}, $F = 17/6$, k_{nn}, $H = 4$, k_{nn}, $D = 4$.
Then substitute average neighbor degree of all above nodes into Formula 2.12, we can obtain:
$k_{nn}(1) = k_{nn}$, $G = 5$
$k_{nn}(2) = (k_{nn}$, $C + k_{nn}$, $H + k_{nn}$, $D)/3 = 9/2$
In a similar manner, we can obtain other $k_{nn}(k)$, and then the distribution of average neighbor degree is shown in Table 2.9.

Table 2.9: Distribution of average neighbor degree of the network shown in Figure 2.1 (b).

k	1	2	3	4	5	6
$k_{nn}(k)$	5	9/2	14/3	0	14/5	17/6

In Table 2.9, $k_{nn}(k)$ tends to decline with increase of k, so the example network in Figure 2.1(b) is in negative correlation, thus the network is disassortative network.

Most social networks are assortative networks, such as scientist coopera-tion network and movie actor/actress cooperation network [19]. Most scientists and movie actors/actresses hope to cooperate with persons at the same level, such that their social network is assortative network. However, many online social networks are disassortative networks. Online social networks shorten the distance among persons, which makes every ordinary people has a chance to easily build one-way friend relationship with "star node" with a larger degree. Figure 2.7 describes the distribution situation of average neighbor degree in Cyworld, an online social network in South Korea, which represents complex nonmonotonous characteristic. We can also see that the overall trend of the average neighbor degree distribution curve is negative. Yong-Yeol Ahn believes that there are different types of users in social networks, and the combination of different types of users leads to the complex distribution of average neigh-bor degree.

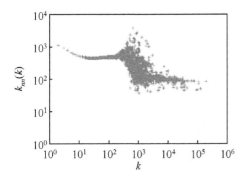

Figure 2.7: Distribution situation of average neighbor degree of Cyworld, an online social network [4].

Alan Mislove et al. [3] found that the distribution function of average neighbor degree of Flickr, LiveJournal, and Orkut tend to increase while that of YouTube tends to decrease. This variation trend indicates that, in YouTube, nodes with larger degrees are more likely to connect those with smaller degrees. As a social network site for video sharing, YouTube certainly has some very popular resource sharing users who can attract other users to connect, and become the star nodes of the network, which is consistent with the characteristics of video sharing. We can roughly determine the assortativity of the network through the trend of the distribution function of average neighbor degree; however, some distribution trends of average neighbor degree in the online social network may be more complex than that shown in Figure 2.7. We will introduce a calculation method below to determine the assortativity of network by substituting the structure information of each node into the formula.

2. Assortativity coefficient

The assortativity coefficient of node r is used to evaluate the relationship between the degree of a node in a network and the degree of its adjacent nodes [19]. The definition is as follows:

$$r = \frac{M^{-1}\sum_i j_i k_i - [M^{-1}\sum_i \frac{1}{2}(j_i + k_i)]^2}{M^{-1}\sum_i \frac{1}{2}(j_i^2 + k_i^2) - [M^{-1}\sum_i \frac{1}{2}(j_i + k_i)]^2} \tag{2.13}$$

where k_i and j_i denote the degree of two nodes connecting with the i edge. M denotes the total number of edges in the network. If the value of r exceeds 0, the degree of the mutual neighbor nodes in the network has positive correlation. Nodes with larger degree tend to connect with each other whereas the adjacent nodes with smaller degree generally have smaller degrees; thus, such networks have assortativity with the corresponding correlation coefficient called the assortativity coefficient. The range of assortativity coefficient is easy to be proved as $0 \le |r| \le 1$. When $r < 0$, the network is disassortative; when $r > 0$, the network is assortative; when $r = 0$, the network is irrelevant, such as the random network.

Substitute the degree sequence of each node in Table 2.2 into Formula 2.13. Its calculation process is as follows:

$$r = \left[\frac{151}{12} - \left(\frac{92}{24}\right)^2\right] / \left[\frac{420}{24} - \left(\frac{92}{24}\right)^2\right] = -0.75$$

In Figure 2.1(b), the assortativity coefficient of Sina Weibo following the network is less than zero ($r < 0$), indicating that the internet is disassortative. This is consistent with our previous conclusion drawn using the distribution of average neighbor degree.

In the early study of complex networks, Newman et al. took the lead in finding that there is assortativity in human social networks, which is different from other biological networks or science and technology networks with disassortativity. Common sense can easily explain the phenomenon: In real life, concerning the needs of social resources, people often want to expand their social circles. Limited to the individual's social classes, it is easy for elites to know each other while ordinary persons can only know similar persons. However, due to the convenience and low cost in social activities in online social networks, which breaks the constraints of human social classes, it is more easy for ordinary people to establish a one-way following or acquaintance with the elites. As related research confirms the law, people find that online social networks generally have characteristics of assortativity or inconspicuous disassortativity (as shown in Table 2.10).

Online social networks' assortativity has an evolutionary process. In the early stage after establishment, social networks usually have assortativity; however, along with the continuous increase of user group scale, many

Table 2.10: Assortativity coefficients of online social networks.

Network	Number of nodes	Assortativity coefficient	Reference	Network	Number of nodes	Assortativity coefficient	Reference
Cyworld	12,048,186	−0.13	[4]	Flickr	1,846,198	0.202	[3]
Nioki	50,259	−0.13	[22]	LiveJournal	5,284,457	0.179	[3]
MySpace	100,000	0.02	[4]	YouTube	1,157,827	-0.033	[3]
Orkut	100,000	0.31	[4]	Mixi	360,802	0.1215	[3]
Xiaonei	396,836	−0.0036	[16]				

networks evolve into disassortativity from assortativity. This is because the early users of social networks are usually introduced by other people who first joined it, such user can restore offline "face-to-face" social relationships vividly. In this stage, the degree correlation of a network node degree represents higher assortativity. However, with the continuous extension and development of the network scale, the site can attract well-known figures, and the original network begins to have excellent users like "opinion leaders," which makes a lot of ordinary users with lower node degree choose to connect these elite users, thus the network evolves into a disassortativity network [17]. Gong et al. [18] studied the link relationship data of the online social network Google+ in several months from the close beta test to open, and found that the assortativity coefficient follows the revolution rule of changing from positive to negative. They think Google+ is a hybrid network consists of two different types of networks, i.e., traditional dating social networks and publish-subscribe networks such as YouTube and Sina Weibo. The former usually has a positive assortativity coefficient while that of the latter may be negative. In the beginning of a close beta test, the traditional dating social networks have superiority, however, the two different types of networks gradually integrated with each other along with lapse of time and increase of users, finally the publish-subscribe networks dominates.

2.4.4 Reciprocity

In general, reciprocity used in a directed network to measure the extent that two nodes in the network form a two-way connection [20]. Research on network reciprocity is of good guidance. On one hand, reciprocity may reflect the closeness of the interaction between individuals in the network; on the other hand, for simplicity in the actual operation, we often ignore the direction of directed edges, while reciprocity can reveal errors caused by ignoring the direction of the edges.

We can use mutual reciprocity coefficient to quantify reciprocity with its mathematical representation as $\varphi = m_d/m$ where m denotes the total number of edges in the network and m_d denotes the number of edges with reverse edges. The real meaning of reciprocal coefficient is very intuitive, i.e., randomly choosing a directed edge from node A to node B from the directed network, then possibility that there is a directed edge from node B to node A. In Figure 2.1(a), Kun Chen → Chen Yao, Zhiying Lin → Degang Guo are unidirectional following relations while the remaining are two-way following relations, so the reciprocity coefficient of the network is $(m-2)/m = 5/6$.

The reciprocity coefficient in dating online social networks are usually higher, for example, reciprocity coefficient of LiveJournal and Flickr is, respectively, 0.74 [4] and 0.68 [21]. In sharing-based microblog networks, there are many celebrity and media nodes with a lot of fans (in-degree) but rare following (out-degree), so reciprocity of microblog are usually poor, for example, reciprocal coefficient of Twitter is only 0.22 [11].

2.5 Social network structure modeling and generation

For social network characteristics discussed in Section 2.4, people often use structure modeling to study the network evolution mechanism of these characteristics. For example, WS model (see Section 2.5.1) introduces the randomness for regular networks by reconnection mechanism, and indicates that such social networks as actor/actress cooperation network and scientific research reference network are substantially a kind of complex between regular network and random network, i.e., small-world network. Through simulating the phenomenon in WWW network that minority webpages indexed by a large number of other web pages, BA model (see Section 2.5.3) promotes the evolution mechanism that nodes tend to establish connections by "preferential attachment" law, and reveals the reason of scale-free characteristics in network. The research on network model is helpful in understanding the formation process of social network and reason for generating some special phenomena, further deepening our understanding of internal law and substantial characteristic of social network.

As a typical complex network, social network, in its network structure and without loss of generality, represents small-world phenomenon and scale-free characteristic of the complex network as well as assortativity, reciprocity, and other characteristics brought by human's social behavior. Through specifically description on network formation process and corresponding instances, this section will thoroughly discuss small-world network model and scale-free network model, and provide an overview of other important networks in Section 2.5.5.

2.5.1 WS model

In 1998, Duncan Watts and Steven Strogatz presented the concept of small-world network and established small-world model, i.e. WS model [24]. As described in Section 2.4.1, the small-world phenomenon reveals characteristics of many complex networks in objective world, i.e., larger average clustering coefficient and shorter average path length. Among them, the shorter average path length is realized through long-distance connection (long-distance connection refers to the connection formed between two nodes with relatively long distance) formed during edge re-connection process.

1. Description of algorithm

Small-world network formed through WS model is the intermediary status of network during the transition from regular network to random network. A network is generated from WS model in the following steps [25]:

(1) We use an annular grid network including n node(s) with node degree of $2k$ as the initial network, and each node in the network is connected to $2k$ node(s) most adjacent to it. Among them, k is an integer larger than zero (usually with small value).

(2) We specify a probability p and reconnect to each edge in the initial network at the probability of p (when reconnecting, randomly choose a node to replace a node connected to such edge). New connection shall not be self-connection and repetitive-connection.

In Step (2), edge connection will generate long-distance connection between two nodes. According to the above process, when $p = 0$, the graph obtained is still original regular network; when $p = 1$, each edge in original graph is randomly re-connected to finally form an approximate random network; when $0 < p < 1$, the original regular network gradually evolves into a small-world network to form an approximate random network.

2. Algorithm example and network generation

At present, most tools provide the algorithm implementation of WS model, such as large-scale complex network analysis tool Pajek[1] , social network research tool SNAP[2] of Stanford University, R language or igraph[3] under Python environment, etc. The following is the code for generating small-world network using SNAP tool with given parameters, and corresponding network structure graph and some statistical characteristic graphs are generated through other integrated open-source tool, including drawing tool Gnuplot and visualization tool Graphviz. After proper environmental configuration, generation, and analysis of the network can be completed by inputting the following code into Python interactive interpreter.

---

1 http://vlado.fmf.uni-lj.si/pub/networks/pajek/.
2 http://snap.stanford.edu/data/.
3 http://igraph.org/redirect.html.

```
1  import snap
2  Rnd = snap.TRnd(1,0)
3  UGraph = snap.GenSmallWorld(N,k,p,Rnd)
4  snap.DrawGViz(UGraph, snap.gvlCirco, "WS.png", "WS small world", False)
5  GraphClustCoeff = snap.GetClustCf(UGraph,-1)
```

where the first line of code is for importing SNAP toolkit; the second line of code generates a random number generator; the third line of code generates a small-world network named as UGraph; the fourth line of code draws UGraph network under gvlCirco layout by invoking open-source tool DrawGViz and save it into a png file named as WS by current operating path, with parameter False indicating no labeling of node serial number in the network. By adjusting parameter N, k, and p in function GenSmallWorld(), scale of the generated network, half of average degree and probability of edge re-connection can be limited accordingly. As shown in Figure 2.8, when N=20, k=2, a group of WS network examples are generated according to different values of p.

where ClustCoeff denotes average clustering coefficient, AvgPathLength denotes average path length. From the first graph, WS small-world network evolves from regular annular grid network to random network as probability of edge re-connection increases from 0 to 1, and average path length changes accordingly as average clustering coefficient decreases. However, we cannot obtain the change law of average clustering coefficient and average path length through just six samplings. The evolution law of average clustering coefficient and average path length after multiple samplings is shown in Figure 2.9.

where $L(0)$ and $C(0)$, respectively, denote average path length and average clustering coefficient of regular network, $L(p)$ and $C(p)$, respectively, denote average path length and average clustering coefficient of the network obtained by edge re-connection at probability p. $L(p)/L(0)$ and $C(p)/C(0)$, respectively, denote the normalization process to $L(p)$ and $C(p)$ by $L(0)$ and $C(0)$. As shown in Figure 2.9, the two parameters show rather different decreasing ratio and law as p increase from 0 to 1: the average path length decreases sharply while average clustering coefficient decreases relatively slow. Therefore, with the proper value of p, the network can have relatively small average length while keeping relatively high average clustering coefficient.

2.5.2 Extension of WS model

Though small-world network with relatively high average clustering coefficient and average path length can be generated in WS model, edge re-connection step therein may harm the connectivity of network and generate some disconnected branches. To remedy this defect, Mark Newman and Duncan Watts modify the "random edge re-connection"

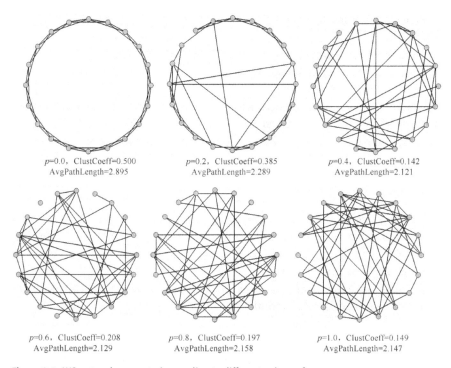

p=0.0，ClustCoeff=0.500
AvgPathLength=2.895

p=0.2，ClustCoeff=0.385
AvgPathLength=2.289

p=0.4，ClustCoeff=0.142
AvgPathLength=2.121

p=0.6，ClustCoeff=0.208
AvgPathLength=2.129

p=0.8，ClustCoeff=0.197
AvgPathLength=2.158

p=1.0，ClustCoeff=0.149
AvgPathLength=2.147

Figure 2.8: WS network generated according to different values of p.

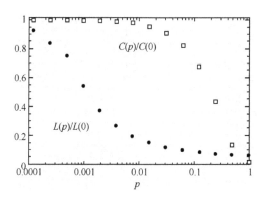

$C(p)/C(0)$

$L(p)/L(0)$

Figure 2.9: Evolution law of average clustering coefficient and average path length [24].

to "random edge addition" [26] and maintain the connectivity of the network by slight modification on original model. The modified model is named as the NW model.

1. Description of algorithm
The establishment process of NW model is as follows:
(1) Similarly, we use an annular grid network including n node(s) as the initial network, and each node in the network is connected to $2k$ node(s) most

adjacent to it. Among them, k is an integer larger than zero (usually with small value).

(2) For each pair of disconnected node (i,j) in the initial network, add an edge e_{ij} between node i and j at the probability of p.

In this process, there is one edge between each node pair at most without self-loop. In this model, when $p = 0$, the generated network is still annular grid network; when $p = 1$, a complete graph forms; when $0 < p < 1$, the sparse regular network evolves into small-world network and finally forms a dense regular network. When network scale n is large enough and p is small enough, the network generated from NW model is basically same as that of WS model.

2. Algorithm example and network generation

NW model may be realized using the method similar to WS model. As shown in Figure 2.10, when $n = 20$, $k = 2$, a group of NW network examples are generated according to different values of p.

Similarly, ClustCoeff denotes average clustering coefficient and AvgPathLength denotes average path length. From the first graph, as probability of edge addition

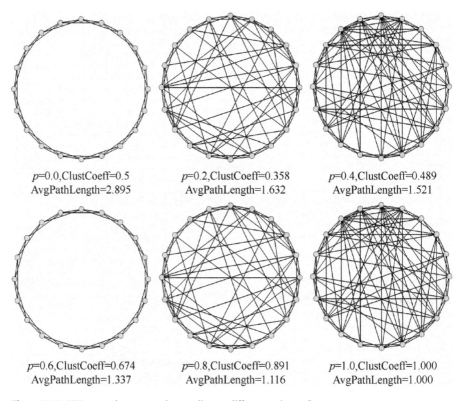

p=0.0,ClustCoeff=0.5
AvgPathLength=2.895

p=0.2,ClustCoeff=0.358
AvgPathLength=1.632

p=0.4,ClustCoeff=0.489
AvgPathLength=1.521

p=0.6,ClustCoeff=0.674
AvgPathLength=1.337

p=0.8,ClustCoeff=0.891
AvgPathLength=1.116

p=1.0,ClustCoeff=1.000
AvgPathLength=1.000

Figure 2.10: NW network generated according to different values of p.

increases from 0 to 1, the network formed has bigger average clustering coefficient and smaller average path length, and the NW small-world network becomes denser and denser. Finally, the initial sparse regular network (annular grid network) forms a dense regular network through small-world network (complete graph).

In addition, WS model and NW model, small-world network has other models, including Monasson small-world network model [27], BW small-world network model [28], among others. Please refer to the relevant reference.

2.5.3 BA model

In traditional random network and small-world network, node degree distribution follows bell-shaped Poisson distribution, i.e., reaching the peak around average and decrease exponentially at two sides. However, according to research on networks in real world, node degree therein follows power-law distribution, i.e., for a randomly specified node in the network, the probability $p(k)$ that it has the degree of k follows $p(k)\sim k^{-\gamma}$, which indicates that large-scale network will self-organize into a scale-free status. Here, scale-free refers to lack of characteristic degree (average degree) in the network, which leads to big fluctuation range. Albert-Laszlo Barabasi and Reka Albert fully explained the phenomenon by simulating resource concentration effect in network through "preferential attachment" mechanism in BA model. Next, we will discuss BA model, an important research result of network structure model research, and other improved extension models.

1. Description and analysis of algorithm
BA model takes into account that network generally has the phenomenon of scale expansion and "the rich becomes richer," i.e., nodes with higher degrees tend to be connected by other nodes and thereby occupy more network resources (higher node degree), promoting two major factors for the network self-organization in scale-free structure.
(1) Network expansion: Network scale is always expanding. For a fully connected network with scale of m_0 at the beginning, add a new node each time and connect it to $m(m \leq m_0)$ existing nodes.
(2) Preferential attachment: The probability Π_i that new nodes connect existing node i depends on the degree k_i of node i, i.e. $\Pi_i = k_i / \sum_j k_j$.
(3) Repeat Step (1) and (2) until the network scale reaches N.
     After time t, there will be $N = t + m_0$ node(s) and mt edge(s) in the network. When t is large enough, m_0 can be omitted to infer that the degree distribution of BA model follows $p(k) \approx 2m^2 k^{-3}$, i.e., power-law distribution. Through mathematical inference, we can obtain the average path length L [29] and average clustering coefficient C [30] of scale-free model:

$$L = \frac{\ln(N)}{\ln\ln(N)}$$

$$C = \frac{m^2(m+1)^2}{4(m-1)} \left[\ln\left(\frac{m+1}{m}\right) - \frac{1}{m+1} \right] \frac{[\ln(t)]^2}{t}$$

In regular network, random network and scale-free network, average path length, and average clustering coefficient have different change laws along with the increase in network scale: the increase in average path length is the fastest in regular network, followed by random network scale-free network; for average clustering coefficient, regular network remains the same, random network decreases the fastest and scale-free network is in the middle.

BA model generates scale-free network by network expansion and "preferential attachment," and lays the foundation for other scale-free network models. In fact, most scale-free network models are the modification or extension version of BA model. The finding of scale-free characteristics and promotion of BA model also create an upsurge of network science research.

2. Algorithm example

To better present the evolution mechanism of BA model, we detail BA model through the generation process of a small-scale network with eight nodes as follows.

Figure 2.11 shows how BA model generates a network, with model parameter as $m_0 = 3$, $m = 2$. There are eight steps as follows from the upper-left to lower-left:
(1) At the beginning, establish a fully connected network with three nodes.
(2) Add a new node in the network.
(3) Connect the new node randomly to two nodes of the existing three nodes. The probability for connecting to each node is equal as existing nodes has the same degree, and can be calculated according to probability formula $\Pi_i = \frac{1}{3}$.
(4) Add another node in the network.

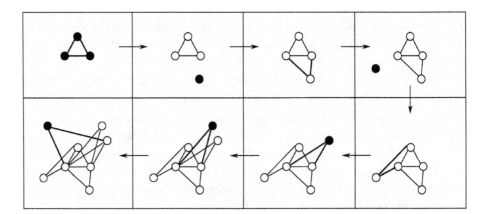

Figure 2.11: The network generation process by BA model.

(5) Connect the new node to two existing nodes according to probability. For the two classes of nodes with degrees of 2 and 3 in Figure 2.11, assuming that the probability to be connected are Π_2 and Π_3 respectively, then $\Pi_2 = \frac{2}{2+2+3+3} = \frac{1}{5}$, $\Pi_3 = \frac{3}{2+2+3+3} = \frac{3}{10}$, i.e., the probability for connecting the new node to two nodes with degree of 3 is higher. In the graph, the "preferential attachment" characteristic of BA model begins to show and become more obvious along with the increase of degree difference between nodes.

(6) Connect the new node to two nodes with the largest degree (the event with the highest probability).

(7) Connect the new node to two nodes with the largest degree (the event with the highest probability).

(8) The probability for connecting the new node to a node with the largest degree is the highest, and to a node with the smallest degree is the lowest. In the subsequent evolution process, degrees of high-degree nodes tend to increase faster and low-degree nodes slower, with a few low-degree nodes evolving into high-degree nodes. The network generated according to the above evolution mechanism can turn into a scale-free network featured by power-law distribution and heavy-tailed phenomenon at the end of evolution.

3. Generation of instance

Use the SNAP tool to generate BA network with a certain scale, and generate network structure graph and statistical characteristic graph by other open-source tools, including drawing tool Gnuplot and visualization tool Graphviz. We will show a network with scale of $N = 500$ and average degree of $k = 1$. After the installation and configuration of tools, input the following code into Python interactive interpreter for network generation and analysis.

```
1  import snap
2  Rnd = snap.TRnd()
3  UGraph = snap.GenPrefAttach(500,1,Rnd)
4  snap.DrawGViz(UGraph, snap.gvlSfdp, "graph generation exp.png", "BA network", False)
5  snap.PlotInDegDistr(UGraph, "Degree distribution", "Degree distribution(BA network)")
```

where the first line of code is for importing SNAP toolkit; the second line of code generates a random number generator; the third line of code generates a undirected BA network named as UGraph; the fourth line of code draws UGraph network under gvlCirco layout by invoking DrawGViz and saves it into a png file named as graph_generation_exp by current operating path, with parameter False indicating that it does not label the serial number of node in the network (see Figure 2.12 for detailed network graph); and the fifth line of code draws the degree distribution graph by invoking open-source tool Gnuplot, as shown in Figure 2.13.

As shown in Figure 2.12, several high-degree nodes occupy most degrees in the network generated by the BA model. As shown in 2.13, degree distribution graph will be a straight line in double logarithmic coordinate, i.e., the generated network follows power-law distribution.

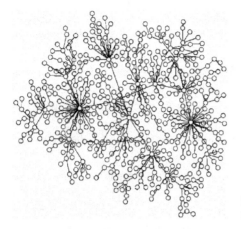

Figure 2.12: Network structure graph of BA scale-free network with 500 nodes.

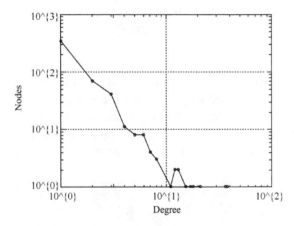

Figure 2.13: Degree distribution graph of BA network.

2.5.4 Extension of BA model

The major contribution of BA scale-free model is that it can precisely depict basic characteristics of most networks, i.e., the expandability of network scale and "preferential attachment" characteristic of new nodes. However, many networks have some special or rather complex characteristics, which have significant effects on actions in network and cannot be depicted in BA model. Therefore, based on BA model, several kinds of extended scale-free network are promoted according to different real networks. We will provide an overview of several important extension versions of BA model, mainly discussing their principles and evolution processes. Please see corresponding reference for more details.

1. EBA model

As described in Section 2.5.3, in BA model, degree distribution $p(k) \sim k^{-\gamma}$ has the power exponent of $\gamma = 3$. However, according to data from real networks, many networks have power exponent of $2 < \gamma < 3$. Based on this situation, Reka Albert and Albert-Laszlo Barabasi extended the original BA model and incorporate "edge re-connection" into the extension version to propose the EBA model [31]. In this model, there are m_0 isolate node(s) at the beginning and one of the following three operations will be carried out each time.

(1) Add $m(m \le m_0)$ edge(s) at probability p. For each edge, choose randomly for one end and at probability of $\Pi(k_i) = \frac{k_i + 1}{\sum_j (k_j + 1)}$ for the other end (preferential connection). Repeat such choosing process for m times to establish m edge(s).

(2) Reconnect m edge(s) at probability q. Each re-connected edge will be generated according to the following rules: Randomly choose a node i and randomly delete an edge l_{ij} connected to it; establish new connection between node i and node j' chosen according to the probability $\Pi(k_{j'})$ in Step (1); repeat this process for m times to form m re-connected edge(s).

(3) Add a new node at probability $1 - p - q$ and establish m edge(s) from this node, with each edge connected to the existing node i at probability $\Pi(k_i)$.

As shown in the above processes, EBA model comprises three main processes: adding node, adding edge, and re-connecting edge. Adding node and adding edge stimulate the network expansion and "preferential attachment," while re-connecting edge stimulates the power exponent controlling power-law distribution. By introducing this simple edge re-connection mechanism, networks generated from EBA model can better fit real networks.

2. Adaptability model

The evolution process of BA model implicitly decides that earlier node has higher node degree, which is quite different from actual situations. For example, influential young people often have more followers in social network, and new innovative websites often attract more users in the internet. These phenomena result from different importance of nodes in the network. Ginestra Bianconi, Albert-Laszlo Barabasi and other researchers introduce the importance of nodes into BA model, which is called as adaptability, and form adaptability model [32]. The detailed processes of adaptability model are as follows:

(1) Network expansion: The network has m_0 node(s) at the beginning, and then adds a new node each time and assigns adaptability $\eta_i (0 < \eta_i < 1)$ for it.

(2) Preferential attachment: Connect the new node to m existing node(s), with the probability Π_i of connecting to an existing node i positively correlated to its node degree k_i and adaptability η_i.

$$\Pi_i = \frac{\eta_i k_i}{\sum_{j=1}^{n} \eta_j k_j}$$

where $n = m_0 + t - 1$ are all nodes existing in the network at $t - 1$.

It is easy to see that after t steps, there will be $n = t + m_0$ node(s) and mt edge(s) in the network. Adaptability model is basically the same as the BA model, except that the probability of "preferential attachment" does not completely rely on node degree by introducing the concept of adaptability. Therefore, if the new node has higher adaptability, it will have higher degree than the existing node with lower adaptability during the network evolution.

3. Generalized linear precedence model

Real network usually have shorter average path length and bigger average clustering coefficient, which are difficult to depict in traditional BA model. To depict average path length and average clustering coefficient on the premise of maintaining scale-free characteristics, Tian et al. [33] promoted generalized linear precedence (GLP) model, which comprises the following steps.

Carry out one of the following operations in a connected network with m_0 node(s) and $m_0 - 1$ edge(s).

(1) Add $m(0 \leq p \leq m_0)$ new edge(s) in the existing network at probability $p(0 \leq p \leq 1)$ and connect one end of each edge to node i at probability $\Pi(k_i) = \frac{k_i - \beta}{\sum_j (k_j - \beta)}$, with k_i as the degree of node i.

(2) Add a new node at probability $1 - p(0 \leq p \leq 1)$ and $m(0 \leq p \leq m_0)$ new edge(s) in the network, and choose the other end i at probability $\Pi(k_i) = \frac{k_i - \beta}{\sum_j (k_j - \beta)}$ for each edge.

where $-\infty < \beta < 1$ is an adjustable parameter, which denotes its tendency of preferentially connecting to a more welcome existing node. When $\beta < 1$, nodes with qa degree of 1 have a chance to obtain new connections. GLP model is able to better match power-law coefficient and average clustering coefficient in real networks.

2.5.5 Other models

Promotion of BA model and WS model changed the dominate status of ER random graph in network modeling, and, along with the deep-going development of network research, people began to realize that complex characteristics in network cannot be depicted and described by a single model. According to the characteristics of different networks, people promote corresponding models to probe their formation mechanisms. These models can be roughly classified into two classes according to the motives of modeling: one class is used to generate network with certain characteristics, such as the abovementioned WS small-world model, NW small-world model, forest-fire model, and Kronecker graph model; the other class is structured for researching the impacts of certain actions on network structure characteristics, such as BA model and its improved models as well as production model. We will provide an overview of these models below. Please refer to the corresponding references for details.

1. Forest-fire model

Jure Leskovec and other researchers [15] found that networks follow the law mentioned below during their research on reference network and coauthor network: in-degree and out-degree follow heavy-tailed distribution, relations between number of nodes and edges (density) follow power-law distribution, and effective diameters of networks decrease along with lapse of time. To simulate and generate networks following these laws, they promoted forest-fire model, through which modeling for directed networks can be performed. During the network evolution process, add one node in network each time and establish several directed edges from such node to existing nodes. When connecting edges, new node v randomly connects to a existing node w, which is called as representative node, then establish a directed edge at certain probability from node v to neighbors of w (including out-neighbor and in-neighbor), expanding layer by layer like forest fire.

Specifically, define two parameters: forward flaming probability p and backward flaming probability r. G_t is an existing network at t, with G_1 having only one node. When adding node v in the network at $t \geq 1$, establish the directed edge from node v to a node in G_t according to the following steps.
(1) First randomly choose a representative node w for node v and establish the directed edge from node v to node w.
(2) Generate a random number x according to binomial distribution with average of $(1-p)^{-1}$, and choose x node(s) for v from neighbors of w, where the proportion for choosing in-neighbor is r times smaller than that of out-degree. Assume the chose nodes as $w_1, w_2, \cdots, w_x$.
(3) Establish the directed edge from node v to nodes $w_1, w_2, \cdots, w_x$, and invoke Step (2) recursively for nodes $w_1, w_2, \cdots, w_x$. During the process, the visited nodes cannot be visited repeatedly so as to avoid from being trapped in loop.

In this model, regardless of the location of representative node in the network, high-degree nodes are more likely connected to new nodes, causing heavy-tailed phenomenon to the in-degree node of network formed. Through recursive invoking during connecting process, a new node forms many out-edges and has big degree, resulting in heavy-tailed phenomenon of out-degree. New nodes in models may establish directed edges through recursion of neighbors of representative nodes, forming community structure in network. New node will form many connections around the community of representative node, granting networks generated from forest-fire model many characteristics observed in real network: heavy-tailed distribution of in-degree and out-degree, power-law distribution of density, decrease in the effective diameter of network along with lapse of time, etc.

2. Kronecker graph model

In generation models simulated on the basis of network properties, some models use the product of matrix to simulate the expansion and evolution of adjacent matrix [34, 5]. Jure Leskovec and other researchers found out that Kronecker product operation of matrix can be used to generate network [36], and verified in experiments that network generated from Kronecker graph model can well simulate the degree distribution of static network, proper value distribution and power-law distribution of diameter and density of dynamic network, etc. Mathematical characteristics of Kronecker product give network generated from Kronecker graph model sound analyzability.

Kronecker product is a kind of matrix product operation. Given matrixes $A = [a_{i,j}]$ in size of $n \times m$ and B in size of $n' \times m'$, then the Kronecker product of matrixes A and B denote a matrix C in size of $(n \cdot n') \times (m \cdot m')$ as follows

$$C = A \otimes B = \begin{pmatrix} a_{1,1}B & a_{1,2}B & \cdots & a_{1,m}B \\ a_{2,1}B & a_{2,2}B & \cdots & a_{2,m}B \\ \vdots & \vdots & \ddots & \vdots \\ a_{n,1}B & a_{n,2}B & \cdots & a_{n,m}B \end{pmatrix}$$

As shown in the above formula, unlike other matrix multiplication, Kronecker product of matrix is extended operation of matrix. Through defining Kronecker product between two graphs as the Kronecker product of their adjacent matrix, these graphs can be expanded into graphs with self-similarity as shown in Figure 2.14.

(1) Run chart K_1 with three nodes.
(2) Middle status of Kronecker product, indicating results after expansion.
(3) Self-Kronecker product results of K_1. K_i denote Kronecker products of i K_1. Specially, K_2 denotes the Kronecker product of two K_1.
(4) Adjacent matrix of K_1.
(5) Adjacent matrix of K_2.

Network generation process of Kronecker graph model is to carry out several times of Kronecker product operation and finally form K_i, It is easy to know that scale of K_i is i power of scale of K_1. According to the mechanism of

Kronecker product, even K_1 with a small scale, like a 3×3 matrix, can finally generate a network with sound variability. To make the model better simulate networks in real world, the author promoted improved mode of Kronecker graph model, i.e., random Kronecker graph model, in which elements in K_1 adjacent matrix is replaced by probability value, making Kronecker graph

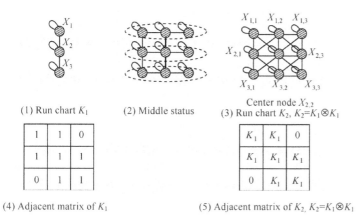

(1) Run chart K_1 (2) Middle status

Center node $X_{2,2}$
(3) Run chart K_2, $K_2=K_1 \otimes K_1$

1	1	0
1	1	1
0	1	1

(4) Adjacent matrix of K_1

K_1	K_1	0
K_1	K_1	K_1
0	K_1	K_1

(5) Adjacent matrix of K_2, $K_2=K_1 \otimes K_1$

Figure 2.14: Kronecker product graphs.

model more flexible. In this manner, the improved model can generate networks with certain characteristics by changing parameters, and also simulate networks in real world by parameter evaluation.

3. Production model

Production model was promoted by Kumar et al. during their observation and research on Flickr and Yahoo!360 network in 2006 [37]. The proposed model simulates directed network and classifies user nodes in the network in three classes: Passive, Linker, and Inviter. Passive node may join the network out of curiosity or from continuous invitations from friends. However, as implied by the name, Passive node acts passively and avoids participating any activity in the network. Inviter node is devoted to moving offline communities to online activities, and thereby continuously invites friends to join the network. Linker node is active participant in network activities and forwardly establishes relationship with other members.

During the network generation process, add one node and ε edge(s) in the network each time and randomly specify the node as one of Passive, Linker, and Inviter. For edges, their classes are related to that of the node. Add each edge in the following steps: Choose a node as the edge source from existing

Inviter node and Linker nodes in the network according to "preferential attachment" rule; in case of Inviter node, add a node in the network as the edge terminal for connection; in case of Linker node, choose a node as the edge terminal from existing Inviter and Linker nodes according to "preferential attachment" rule.

Network generated by this model conforms to characteristics observed in Flickr and Yahoo!360, i.e., nodes in network are classified into three classes: inactive node with degree of zero (isolate node), huge branches with strong connection internal and all kinds of isolate small communities. Among them, isolate communities are basically in star topology structure, which expand fast at first and merge into a huge branch or stop expanding later. In huge branches, average distance between node decreases along with lapse of time. During network evolution process, new nodes and connections continuously appear. Increase of nodes directly leads to expansion of network scale while increase of edges may lead to the merger of two separated parts in the network. Along with the lapse of time, network scale changes and different branches merge, however, the proportions of the three parts in the network basically remain the same.

2.6 Summary

In this chapter, we considered social network structure as the research object. Based on the important characteristics of social network, we detailed several important structure parameters of social network, i.e., degree distribution, average path length, and so on, and performed detailed analysis on small-world phenomenon, scale-free characteristic, assortativity, and other structural characteristics of social network, which are different from other complex networks. Based on this, we introduced the establishment method of WS small-world model, BA scale-free model, forest-fire model, Kronecker graph model, production model, and other traditional social network structure models. The principal goal of establishing social network structure model is to research the generation mechanism of certain network structures and some network properties, and, in the second place, conveniently and economically provide simulation data from real network for researches in other fields. Structure characteristic research on social network is the basis of researches on other aspects and its continuous development significantly promoted social network science as well as complex network science.

Research and analysis on online social network is one of the fields first attended to and fully explored. During 2005 to 2010, structure characteristic work based on real social network data is active, covering online social networks home and abroad from familiar Flickr and Livejournal to uncommon Cyworld and Wealink, from foreign

Twitter and Facebook to domestic Sina Weibo and Xiaonei. These works enable us to fully recognize the similarity and characteristics of different online social networks, and obtain a series of parameters available for describing network structure characteristic. In recent years, research only focusing on network structure becomes rare along with applying results in earlier stages to other subsequent research fields, such as node impact prediction by network structure parameters by applying statistical methods, time length prediction on information dissemination.

References

[1]   Mayhew B, Levinger R: Size and the density of human interaction in social aggregates. *Am J Sociol* 1976, 82:86–110.
[2]   Wang X, Li X, Chen G: Complex network theory and its application. Beijing: Tsinghua University Press, 2006.
[3]   Mislove A, Marcon M, Gummadi KP, Druschel P, Bhattacharjee B: Measurement and analysis of online social networks. In Proceedings of the 7th ACM SIGCOMM conference on Internet measurement. ACM, 2007: 29–42.
[4]   Ahn YY, Han S, Kwak H, Moon S, Jeong H: Analysis of topological characteristics of huge online social networking services. In Proceedings of the 16th international conference on World Wide Web. ACM, 2007: 835–844.
[5]   Milgram S. The small world problem. *Psychol Today* 1967, 2:60–67.
[6]   Backstrom L, Boldi P, Rosa M, Ugander J, Vigna S: Four degrees of separation. ArXiv. Retrieved 23 November 2011.
[7]   Barabasi AL, Albert R: Emergence of scaling in random networks. *Science* 1999, 286:509–512.
[8]   Erdös P, Rényi A: On random graphs I. *Publ Math Debrecen* 1959, 6:290–297.
[9]   Karl S: Appendix: A primer on heavy-tailed distributions. *Queueing Syst* 1999, 33:261–275.
[10] Clauset C, Shalizi C, Newman M: Power-law distributions in empirical data. *SIAM Rev* 2009, 51:661–703.
[11] Kwak H, Lee C, Park H, Moon S: What is Twitter, a social network or a news media?. In Proceedings of the 19th international conference on World wide web. ACM, 2010: 591–600.
[12] Ravasz E, Barabasi AL: Hierarchical organization in complex networks. *Phys Rev E* 2003, 67:026112.
[13] Wilson C, Boe B, Sala A, Puttaswamy KP, Zhao BY: User interactions in social networks and their implications. In Proceedings of the 4th ACM European conference on Computer systems. ACM, 2009: 205–218.
[14] Fu F, Chen X, Liu L, Wang L: Social dilemmas in an online social network: The structure and evolution of cooperation. *Phys Lett A* 2007, 371:58–64.
[15] Leskovec J, Kleinberg J, Faloutsos C: Graphs over time: densificationlaws, shrinking diameters and possible explanations. In Proceedings of ACM SIGKDD, pages 177–187, Chicago, Illinois, USA, 2005. ACM Press.
[16] Fu F, Liu L, Wang L: Empirical analysis of online social networks in the age of web 2.0. *Physica A* 2008, 387:675–684.
[17] Hu H, Wang X: Evolution of a large online social network. *Phys Lett A* 2009, 373:1105–1110.
[18] Gong NZ, Xu W, Huang L, Mittal P, Stefanov E, Sekar V, Song D: Evolution of social-attribute networks: measurements, modeling, and implications using google+. In Proceedings of the 2012 ACM conference on Internet measurement conference. ACM, 2012: 131–144.

[19] Newman M, Forrest S, Balthrop J: Email networks and the spread of computer viruses. *Phys Rev E* 2002, 66:035101.

[20] Garlaschelli D, Loffredo MI: Patterns of link reciprocity in directed networks. *Phys Rev Lett* 2004, 93:268701.

[21] Cha M, Mislove A, Gummadi KP: A measurement-driven analysis of information propagation in the flickr social network. In Proceedings of the 18th international conference on World wide web. ACM, 2009: 721–730.

[22] Holme P, Edling CR, Liljeros F: Structure and time evolution of an Internet dating community. *Soc Netw* 2004, 26:155–174.

[23] Li Y: Topological characteristics analysis of online social network. Complex System and Complexity Science, 2012.

[24] Watts JD, Strogatz HS: Collective dynamics of 'small-world'networks. Nature, 1998, 393: 440–442.

[25] Wang XF, Chen G: Complex networks: Small-world, scale-free and beyond. Circ Syst Mag IEEE 2003, 3:6–20.

[26] Newman M, Watts DJ: Renormalization group analysis of the small-world network model. *Phys Lett A* 1999,263:341–346

[27] Newman M: The structure and function of complex networks. *SIAM Rev* 2003, 45:167–256.

[28] Boccaletti S, Latora V, Moreno Y, Chavez M, Huang DU: Complex networks: Structure and dynamics. *Phys Rep* 2006, 424:175–308.

[29] Cohen R, Havlin S: Scale-free networks are ultrasmall. *Phys Rev Lett* 2003, 90:058701.

[30] Fronczak A, Fronczak P, Holyst J: Mean-field theory for clustering coefficients in Barabasi-Albert networks. arXiv preprint cond-mat/0306255, 2003.

[31] Albert R, Barabasi AL Topology of evolving networks: Local events and universality. *Phys Rev Lett* 2000, 85:5234.

[32] Bianconi C, Barabasi AL: Bose-Einstein condensation in complex networks. *Phys Rev Lett* 2001, 86:5632.

[33] Bu T, Towsley D: On distinguishing between Internet power law topology generators. INFOCOM 2002. Twenty-First Annual Joint Conference of the IEEE Computer and Communications Societies. Proceedings. IEEE. IEEE, 2002, 2: 638–647.

[34] Chakrabarti D, Zhan Y, Faloutsos C R-MAT: A recursive model for graph mining. *SDM* 2004, 4:442–446.

[35] Leskovec J, Faloutsos C: Scalable modeling of real graphs using kronecker multiplication. In Proceedings of the 24th international conference on Machine learning. ACM, 2007: 497–504.

[36] Leskovec J, Chakrabarti D, Kleinberg J, Faloutsos C, Ghahramani Z: Kronecker graphs: An approach to modeling networks. *J Mach Learn Res* 2010, 11:985–1042.

[37] Kumar R, Novak J, Tomkins A: Structure and evolution of online social networks. In Proceedings of the 12th ACM SIGKDD international conference on Knowledge discovery and data mining. ACM, 2006: 611–617.

[38] Leskovec J, Horvitz E: Planetary-scale views on a large instant-messaging network. In Proceedings of the 17th international conference on World Wide Web. ACM, 2008: 915–924.

[39] Golbeck J: Analyzing the social web. Newnes, 2013.

Jianhua Li

3 Technologies and approaches for virtual community detection

3.1 Introduction

Along with the development of communications and computer technology, social network now serves as an important platform for daily communication, personal life show, and distributing messages. The relationships among social network users are uneven. Some individuals have dense relationships whereas others have sparse relationships, forming the virtual community structure in social networks. Detecting the community structure in social networks helps in understanding the characteristics of the topological structure of network, revealing the intrinsic characteristics of complex systems and comprehending the relationships/behaviors of individuals as well as its evolution, thus providing strong support for information retrieval, information recommendation, information propagation control, organization management, public safety incidents control, and many other applications. Virtual community detection in social network has both important theoretical value and great practical significance. In recent years, research on algorithms for virtual community detection has attracted considerable attention from scholars. A series of classic community detection algorithms have been proposed for mining virtual communities in social networks of different sizes. Moreover, with the increase in the social network size and node information, community detection algorithms are trying to achieve high accuracy while reducing the time complexity and pay more attention to the local topological structure of social networks.

This chapter will introduce virtual community detection algorithms, including the evaluation system of these algorithm and some classic algorithms for community detection. This chapter is organized as follows: first, Section 3.2 presents the definition of virtual community and development process of community detection algorithms, and introduces the evaluation system of the algorithms considering the two aspects of evaluation accuracy and computation complexity. Second, according to the different computation processes of objective functions in the community detection algorithms, we classify the algorithms into two classes and describe them. Section 3.3, from the perspective of static computation, introduces some classic static community detection algorithms such as modularity optimization algorithms, multiobjective optimization algorithms, and algorithms based on probability model and information coding algorithms. Section 3.4, from the perspective of dynamic computation, introduces some classic dynamic algorithms such as cluster percolation algorithms, agglomerative algorithms based on similarity, label propagation algorithms, and local expansion optimization algorithms.

https://doi.org/10.1515/9783110599374-003

3.2 Theoretical basis of virtual community detection technology

3.2.1 The definition of virtual community

In the 1970s, many scholars began to realize that there are some node sets with closely-connected nodes in many graphs These sets significatly influence the topological structure of the entire graph. Therefore, people started to use mathematical tools, such as graph theory, to detect these node sets as the problem of graph partitioning and defined these sets as subgraph with the characteristic of close connection. Along with the gradual improvement and deepening of the complex network theory, scholars realized that node sets with the characteristic of local close connection also exist in complex networks and proposed the concept of community. Mark Newman and other complex system scientists tried to reveal and expound such community structures by some theories of complex networks. In recent years, online social network has progressed tremendously as a new type of complex network, wherein nodes in the virtual network map people in the real society and network edges denote the exchange and communication between network users. At present, the problem of community detection in online social networks has attracted much attention. As online social networks can be regarded as a virtual environment platform different from the real world, community can also be called a virtual community. So far, people have given many different definitions of the community (virtual community) from different aspects, including the local definition based on subgraph, the global definition based on network modularity, as well as definitions based on the similarity between nodes.

1. Local definition based on subgraph

Community structure can be regarded as several node sets with high cohesion in the network topology. These sets are usually abstraction of relatively independent components with independent functions or properties. Therefore, the community structure can be defined according to the characteristics of local network topology. So far, a descriptive definition accepted by scholars in various fields is the local definition based on subgraph, i.e., community structures are several subsets of the node sets in a complex network. The connections between nodes in each subset are relatively compact whereas the connected edges between nodes in different subsets are relatively sparse. In Figure 3.1, 20 nodes in the network are partitioned into three community structures, with each corresponding to the structure in three dotted circles. In these three communities, nodes are closely connected to each other whereas edges between communities are relatively sparse.

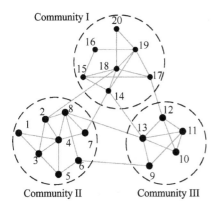

Figure 3.1: A small network with virtual community structure.

2. Global definition based on the network modularity

To evaluate the community structure, Newman et al. proposed the definition of modularity [1] by simulating the definition of variance according to the differences between topological structures of real and random networks. Modularity can be defined as the expected difference between the ratio of edges between nodes in the same class (edges in the same community) and the ratio of edges between these nodes of random connections in the same community structure. According to this definition, higher modularity results in better community structure. Modularity can evaluate community structure through the global information in topological structures of networks. This community definition based on modularity is often applied in community detection algorithms to evaluate the community structure or provide stop condition for the algorithm.

3. Definition based on the similarity between nodes

In physical sense, communities usually denote a set of elements in complex systems or networks with the same or similar function. These elements collaborate or interact with each other, completing some relatively independent functions in the entire system or forming some relatively independent organizational structures. As a result, communities can be defined based on the similarities between nodes. This definition assumes that nodes in the community are similar, while the similarity between nodes in different communities is low. Certain indexes should be used to evaluate the similarity between network nodes for further defining the community structure.

In general, from the aspect of essential meaning, all existing definitions of community (virtual community) are consistent, i.e., for a subset of the set comprised by all individuals in networks, individuals therein are closely connected based on certain properties and have sparse connections with individuals out of the subset.

3.2.2 Development process of virtual community detection

Algorithms

Essentially, virtual community detection in online social networks can be regarded as the procedure of partitioning the network nodes into several subgraphs according to the closeness in topological structure. In computer science, such problems are often regarded as graph partitioning problem. Research on graph partitioning problem dates back to the 20th century, among which two most important algorithms are Kernighan-Lin algorithm [2] and the spectral bisection algorithm [3]. Kernighan-Lin algorithm, based on greedy optimization strategy, defines an objective revenue function and seeks the best partitioning through which the objective revenue function can achieve the maximum value by greedy search. Kernighan-Lin can not only find the reasonable partitioning of network but also show the community structure by tree diagram, revealing the hierarchical community structure. The spectral bisection algorithm starts from the Laplacian matrix of network and implements dichotomy on the network topological structure by researching the eigenvalue and eigenvector of the matrix. Community partition with the number of community greater than 2 can be obtained by applying the algorithm iteratively. In the 21st century, along with the development of complex network science, the problem of network community structure detection has attracted increasing attention of scholars from different fields. Michelle Girvan and Mark Newman proposed a new splitting algorithm in 2002, i.e., the GN algorithm [4]. In the algorithm, they proposed the concept of modularity to evaluate community structure based on the comparison between the structural characteristics of complex networks and random networks, initiating the fruitful development of community detection. GN algorithm, essentially a kind of network splitting algorithm, identifies edges between communities through customized edge betweenness and removes the edge with the biggest edge betweenness, thus splitting the network into several virtual communities. Furthermore, Newman et al. found that optimizing the objective function modularity helps to better detect community structure, as modularity is an important index to evaluate the community partition. Inspired by this idea, many scholars considered modularity as an objective function and proposed several community detection algorithms [20] based on the optimization of modularity function. Considering essential deficiency in the modularity function, Shi et al. proposed the community detection algorithm based on multi-objective optimization. They described the community structure characteristics accurately and comprehensively with multi-objectives function and realized the optimization of objective function to detect the community structure in network. For applications needing detailed description of community structure, experts in the field of information science, from the aspect of information theory, mapped the network topological structure into the data coding problem and achieved community detection by constructing the community partition with the shortest coding length. A typical example is Infomap algorithm, which can detect communities in networks more accurately and is often applied when accurate analysis for community structure is needed [5]. Considering the phenomenon that several nodes in networks belong to multiple communities at the same time, Palla et al. proposed the concept of overlapping community in 2005 and tried to detect overlapping communities in networks and bridge nodes along the boundary of communities based on the definition of clique [6]. By investigating the differences in topology characteristics between real networks and virtual networks through mathematical tools such as Bayesian inference, Newman et al. proposed the community detection algorithm based on the probability model and detected overlapping communities using the maximization of the likelihood probability. All the algorithms mentioned above place more emphasis on the accuracy of community structure while pay less attention to the time complexity, thus the time complexity is often relatively high. Consequently, these algorithms are only fit for virtual community detection in social networks with a small size. In fact, it is often necessary to analyze virtual communities in social networks with large-scale and wide range of node information, requiring the community detection algorithm to have high accuracy and low time complexity. Considering requirements of both the above aspects, scholars have proposed some new community detection algorithms form different perspectives for accurate and rapid detection of virtual communities in large-scale social networks. Scholars researched local structure characteristics of community structures and proposed several community detection algorithms based on local expansion. This kind of algorithms often starts from one or several core nodes in the network, define the local objective function, and absorb surrounding nodes into existing virtual community structure by greedy strategy. As this kind of algorithms only uses the local topological structure of network, it is capable of detecting and analyzing the community structure in the area concerned before constructing topological structure diagram of the entire network [7]. To improve the efficiency of community detection in networks, Raghavan et al. discussed a community detection algorithm based on label propagation [8]. The algorithm provides a unique label for each node, and iteratively updates the label value of a node according to the majority labels of its neighbors. Finally, the procedure converges into the stable status with some nodes sharing the same label in the network, which are nodes belong to the same community. This kind of algorithms can detect the network community structure in linear time when the topological structure of the entire network is known.

3.2.3 The accuracy indexes of evaluation for virtual community detection algorithms

So far, various kinds of algorithms have been proposed for community detection. Different algorithms may partition the same network into different community structures. It is a big challenge to evaluate those community structures partitioned by different algorithms. For this purpose, researchers proposed digital evaluation indexes [9] to measure the accuracy of community detection algorithms, such as modularity and NMI.

1. Modularity

Mark Newman proposed the modularity index to measure the differences in community structure by comparing the connection density differences between existing networks and reference networks under the same community partitioning, with reference network as the random network with the same degree sequence as the original network. Assume that A denotes the adjacent matrix of a complex network and k_v denotes the degree of node v, i.e., $k_v = \sum_w A_{vw}$. In corresponding reference network, the probability of existence of edge (v, w) is $\frac{k_v k_w}{2m}$, with m as the number of edges in network graph A. Then the complete mathematical expression of modularity is shown in Formula 3.1:

$$Q = \frac{1}{2m} \sum_{vw} \left[A_{vw} - \frac{k_v k_w}{2m} \right] \delta(c_v, c_w) \tag{3.1}$$

where c_v denotes the community which v belongs to. If $i = j$, $\delta(i, j) = 1$; otherwise $\delta(i, j) = 0$. Mathematically, Formula 3.1 denotes the expectation difference between the ratio of edges in the same community and the ratio of edges in reference network under the same community structure. Higher modularity brings better community partitioning in complex networks. To calculate the modularity Q more conveniently, use the following Formula 3.2. Assume that the complex network is partitioned into k community structures and define a symmetric matrix e (e_{ij}) with $k \times k$ order, where e_{ij} denotes the ratio of edges between two communities i and j to all edges of the network. The sum of all elements on the diagonal denotes the ratio of edges between nodes in the same community to all edges of the entire network, expressed by $\mathrm{Tre} = \sum_i e_{ii}$. The sum of elements in each row is expressed by $\mathrm{Tre}\ a_i = \sum_j e_{ij}$, which denotes the ratio of edges connected to nodes in community i to edges of the entire network.

Based on the definition above, Formula 3.1 can be transformed into Formula 3.2 as:

$$Q = \sum_i (e_{ii} - a_i^2) = \mathrm{Tre} - ||e^2|| \tag{3.2}$$

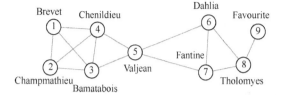

Figure 3.2: Relationships between some characters in Les Miserables.

where $\|e\|$ denotes the sum of all elements in matrix e. More obvious community structure in complex networks results in bigger modularity Q. In real networks, the value range of modularity is often 0.3~0.7.

Taking Figure 3.2 for example, the computation process can be introduced as follows. The figure is an abstraction reflecting the relationships between some characters in Les Miserables, where node 1, node 2, node 3, and node 4 denote the characters related to the Champmathieu case, while node 6, node 7, node 8, and node 9 denote characters centered by Fantine, mother of the daughter adopted by Valjean. The adjacent matrix corresponding to the figure is expressed as follows:

$$A = \begin{pmatrix} 0 & 1 & 1 & 1 & 0 & 0 & 0 & 0 & 0 \\ 1 & 0 & 1 & 1 & 0 & 0 & 0 & 0 & 0 \\ 1 & 1 & 0 & 1 & 1 & 0 & 0 & 0 & 0 \\ 1 & 1 & 1 & 0 & 1 & 0 & 0 & 0 & 0 \\ 0 & 0 & 1 & 1 & 0 & 1 & 1 & 0 & 0 \\ 0 & 0 & 0 & 0 & 1 & 0 & 1 & 1 & 0 \\ 0 & 0 & 0 & 0 & 1 & 1 & 0 & 1 & 0 \\ 0 & 0 & 0 & 0 & 0 & 1 & 1 & 0 & 1 \\ 0 & 0 & 0 & 0 & 0 & 0 & 0 & 1 & 0 \end{pmatrix}$$

Assume that, through a certain algorithm, the network can be partitioned into three communities: $c_1=\{1, 2, 3, 4\}$, $c_2=\{5\}$, $c_3=\{6, 7, 8, 9\}$. $m = 14$ denotes the number of edges in the figure. The modularity component of community c_1 is 0.1786, the modularity component of community c_2 is 0 and the modularity component of community c_3 is 0.1581, with total modularity degree of 0.3367.

Although the modularity proposed by Mark Newman can evaluate the community partitioning accurately, as recognized by many specialists and scholars, there are still several problems in modularity indexes. For example, Fortunato et al. found that the partitioning corresponding to the modularity maximum is not necessarily the best community partitioning result. Under many circumstances, there is a potential scale of the smallest community, and any community structure with a scale smaller than such potential will have a negative effect on the modularity optimization.

2. NMI

Along with the development of online social networks, people realized that several online social networks have information implying the community membership of each node. For example, the school information on renren. com reveals the community structure of nodes from the same school and the interest information on Facebook characterizes virtual user groups with the same interests. These data provides rich information for virtual community detection as well as the standard answer for evaluating virtual community structure. In case that some virtual community structure information is known in advance, Danon et al. proposed the normalized mutual information (NMI), which evaluates the differences between the community structure partitioned by the algorithm and the known community structure [10]. NMI is a digital index calculated by confusion matrix N. Given two community partitions: $a = (a_1, a_2, \cdots, a_n)$, $b = (b_1, b_2, \cdots, b_n)$, where a_p, $b_p(p = 1, 2, \cdots, n)$ denotes the number of community which node p belongs to in these two partitions and n denotes the number of nodes in the network. NMI formula is as follows:

$$\text{NMI} = \frac{-2 \sum_{i,j} N_{ij} \ln\left(\frac{N_{ij} n}{N_{i.} N_{.j}}\right)}{\sum_{i} N_{i.} \ln\left(\frac{N_{i.}}{n}\right) + \sum_{j} N_{j.} \ln\left(\frac{N_{.j}}{n}\right)} \quad (3.3)$$

where N_i denotes the sum of elements in row i of the matrix N and N_j denotes the sum of elements in column j of matrix N.

This numeric index can be used to evaluate the difference between the detected community structure and known structure. Higher value results in better partitioning of community structure. If the value reaches the maximum of 1, the community structure detected by the algorithm is the same as the known structure and the result of the algorithm is the best.

With the example of Figure 3.2, the computation procedure of NMI is shown as follows. Assume that the best known community structure partitioning can be expressed as {1, 2, 3, 4}, {5} and {6, 7, 8, 9}. The vector of community partitioning is a = (1, 1, 1, 1, 2, 3, 3, 3, 3). Then assume that the community structure partitioned by a certain algorithm can be denoted by vector b = (3, 3, 3, 3, 2, 1, 1, 1, 1).

According to the known community partition vector, the confusion matrix N can be constructed as follows:

$$N = \begin{pmatrix} 0 & 0 & 4 \\ 0 & 1 & 0 \\ 4 & 0 & 0 \end{pmatrix}$$

According to Formula 3.3, the NMI value of this partitioning is 1.

3. Rand index

Virtual community detection problems in online social networks can be regarded as the problem of clustering in the field of data mining. Except for the NMI numeric index, scholars in data mining field have described other numeric indexes to evaluate clustering results, of which Rand index is a typical example [11]. Rand index indicates the ratio of the number of node pairs which belong to the same community or different communities in the two partitions. Assume that n nodes are denoted by $X_1, X_2, \cdots, X_n$ in two partitioning, i.e., Y and Y', the Rand index can be calculated as follows:

$$R(Y, Y') = \sum_{i<j}^{n} \gamma_{ij} / C_n^2 \tag{3.4}$$

where C_n^2 denotes the number of probable node pairs of the n nodes, i.e., $(n-1)n/2$. If node X_i and X_j are partitioned into the same community or different communites in both two partitioning, $\gamma_{ij} = 1$; otherwise, if the node X_i and X_j are partitioned into the same class in one partitioning but partitioned into different communties in another partitioning, $\gamma_{ij} = 0$.

The computation procedure can also be illustrated by Figure 3.2. Assume that there are two partitioning {{1, 2, 3, 4}, {5}, 6, 7, 8, 9}} and {{1, 2, 3, 4, 5}, {6, 7, 8, 9}}. According to the definition of γ_{ij}, 12 node pairs are partitioned into the same class in both partitionings, and 20 pairs are partitioned into different classes in both the partitionings. There are 36 node pairs in total, so the Rand index of these two partitioning is 8/9. If these two partitionings are the same, the value is 1 and results of the algorithm is the best. For its simple calculation in definition, this index is capable of effectively evaluating the partition results of virtual communities in online social networks of large scale.

An improvement for Rand index is Mirkin with the following formula:

$$M(X, Y) = n(n-1)[1 - R(X, Y)] \tag{3.5}$$

4. Jaccard index

Jaccard index is a numeric index similar to Rand index with the following formula:

$$J(x, y) = \frac{a_{11}}{a_{11} + a_{01} + a_{10}} \tag{3.6}$$

where a_{11} denotes the number of pairs partitioned into the same subset in both partitioning while a_{01} and a_{10} denote the number of pairs partitioned into the same community in one partitioning but partitioned into different communities in another partitioning. We introduce the computation process of Jaccard index with the example in Figure 3.2. Considering two kinds of partitioning: {{1, 2, 3, 4}, {5}, {6, 7, 8, 9}} and $\{\{1, 2, 3, 4, 5\}, \{6, 7, 8, 9\}\}$ with $a_{11} = 12$ and $a_{11} + a_{01} + a_{10} = 16$, then $J(x, y) = 12/16 = 0.75$.

3.2.4 The computational complexity of algorithms for virtual community detection

To evaluate a community detection algorithm, we should consider its computational complexity in addition to its accuracy in partitioning. In terms of the computational complexity of algorithms, the amount of resources required for the task mainly depends on the time complexity and space complexity.

In general, time complexity of an algorithm is the function of computation effort for executing the algorithm, which describes the run time of the algorithm quantitatively. In general, we use the symbol O to denote the function, which provides the maximum of the run time. In this manner, the expression denotes the time magnitude needed for the algorithm when the input tends to infinite, without any lower order terms and leading coefficients.

Space complexity measures temporary memory space needed for the algorithm at run time, which is usually the function of problem scale. In the field of virtual community detection, we usually denote the problem scale as the number of nodes or edges in the network. Similar to time complexity, we use O to denote the scale function of space complexity for the problem in space complexity.

3.2.5 Typical datasets needed for testing virtual community detection algorithms

To test the performance of the community detection algorithms, many scholars in various fields, especially sociology, have carried out modeling and abstraction for complex systems in different fields, and have extracted many topological reference graphs with typical community structure. Centered on the detection problem of community structure, typical datasets can be classified into two classes: real reference network and artificial reference network.

1. Real reference network
Real reference network is an abstraction of real social networks with obvious community structure, thus the community structure there usually has specific practical meaning. The network of Zachary's karate club is the most cited in the research area of current community detection algorithms for social network, which reflects the social relationship between members in the karate club [12]. In the early 1970s, Zachary observed the relationship between members of a karate club in a college in America for two years. In this graph, Zachary club members are denoted by nodes and social

relationships by edges between nodes in the network, thereby constructing the relationship network of the club, as shown in Figure 3.3. In the network, 34 nodes denote 34 members and edges between nodes denote friendship between them. Within two years after Zachary constructs this network graph, the club administrator (node 1) and the instructor (node 33) broke up on whether to raise the fee of the club, and the club split into two communities centered on the club administrator and the instructor. These two communities provide good results evaluation basis for partitioning virtual community in social network and cited by many scholars. However, this network has only 34 nodes, which is its main deficiency. In the 21st century, scholars from various fields have tried to find a network with larger scale and thereby detect virtual

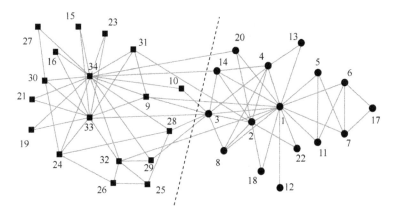

Figure 3.3: Topological structure of Zachary's karate club network.

community structure. Newman et al. analyzed and sorted the schedule arrangements between teams of MLS, thereby extracting the NCAA football network with the topological structure of the network, as shown in Figure 3.4. In the NCAA football network, there are 115 nodes denoting the teams and each edge denotes one or several matches played between two teams. These 115 teams are partitioned into 12 communities according to the states they belong to with more matches played between teams in each community and less matches played between teams between communities, forming a natural community structure.

The development of online social networks provides considerable data for research on virtual community detection algorithms. Scholars realized that many characteristics in online social networks reflect the social relationship in real world with many special topological properties. These properties have significant influence on the virtual community structure of online social networks, through which many scholars collect the information in many online social networks as the practical test data for virtual communities. The dataset of blog network of U.S. politicians is a

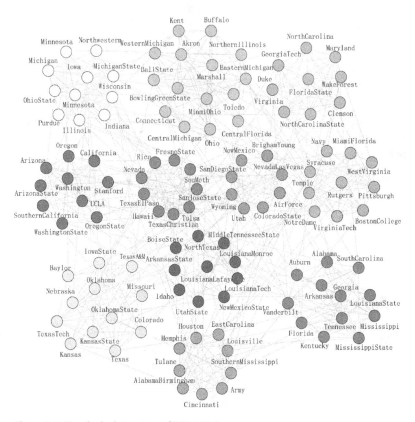

Figure 3.4: Topological structure of NCAA MLS.

typical example. The dataset includes 1,491 nodes and each node denotes a virtual ID on a famous blog. During the U.S. presidential election 2004, users on the blog are partitioned into conservatives and liberals according to their different political stands, leading to the obvious communities in the network. Figure 3.5 shows the community structure formed by part of nodes in the network which are partitioned into two communities according to their different political preferences and marked in black and grey respectively. The dataset collected from a famous online social site in U.S. intuitively reflects the essential features of community structure in the network. The Blog network based on MSN, an online chatting tool, is another typical example. Each user on MSN is denoted by a node in the network. The edge between two nodes can be constructed if the comment behavior between them is frequent. After several times of data collecting, the Blog network includes 30,557 nodes and 82,301 edges. In this network, account nodes with same interests have more mutual comments. As a result, the network reveals the virtual community structure marked by topics of interest. Along with the rapid development of online social networks like Facebook, many scientists collect the data therein and analyze the virtual community

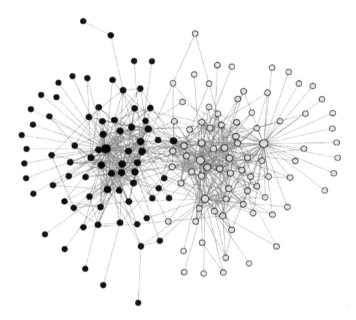

Figure 3.5: Blog network of U.S. politicians.

structure of such networks. Traud et al. construct the social network among students in a university in U.S. according to the similar relation of users [41]. The network includes 769 nodes and 16,656 edges which are partitioned into several virtual community structures according to the friendship among users.

The relationship network of characters in Les Misérables introduced in Section 3.2.3 in this chapter is also a simple social network. As shown in Figure 3.6, 9 nodes in the network are partitioned into two communities. One community, based on Champmathieu case, is related characters interrogated instead of him after Champmathieu was mistaken for Valjean. The other community centers on Fantine which includes the social relationships among Fantine and people who abandoned her. Valjean, as the prolabelonist, is related to all the nodes in the network and can be regarded as the node in the overlapping region.

2. Artificial reference network

Real reference networks are abstraction of systems in the real world, and communities therein usually have certain background meaning. Systems are often affected by various factors in real world, hence, the community structure therein does not completely conform to the definition of community. To solve this problem, many

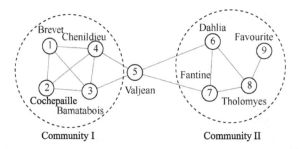

Figure 3.6: Network of character relationships in Les Miserables.

experts and scholars in complex science and sociology constructed artificial network reference graph model based on the power-law distribution characteristic of node degree and the small-world phenomenon in complex networks. Without the influence of external factors in real world, the community structure in artificial network is more distinct and reasonable, providing a powerful means for evaluating community detection algorithms. Two famous network models in artificial reference network are GN artificial network proposed by Newman et al. and LFR artificial network proposed by Lancichinetti et al. [13]. These two artificial networks both dynamically generate networks in specified node scale and with typical community structure based on the topological characteristics of complex networks with the number of nodes as parameter. As a result, they are suitable for constructing online social networks of large scale. GN artificial network, proposed by Mark Newman, partitions nodes in the network partitioned into different communities with the number of nodes in the network, number of communities, and the edge distribution of each node as its input parameters. Degrees of each node, the number of edges inside the same community and other information decide the community that a node belongs to and the clarity of the entire network community structure. Figure 3.7 is a network topological structure graph with 128 nodes generated from GN artificial network, which is partitioned into 4 communities with 32 nodes in each community and each node therein has the degree 16.

Although GN artificial network can simulate networks with community structure to a certain extent, each community has the same number of nodes because of the uniform partition of nodes into specified communities. This deficiency leads to big difference in topological properties between network generated from GN artificial networks and real complex networks. To address this problem, Lancichinetti et al. proposed the LFR reference network model. Compared with GN artificial network, the LFR artificial network needs more input parameters and better conforms to the real online social networks in topological properties owing to better flexibility of topological structure reference network constructed by it. In LFR artificial network, users can set parameters to control the entire network and topological properties of each community, such as community scale, degree distribution of nodes and the ratio

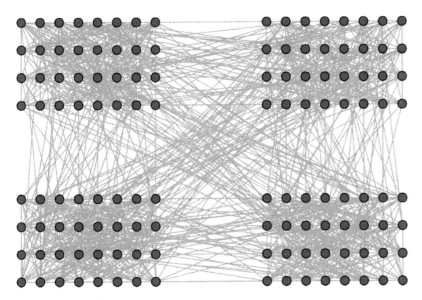

Figure 3.7: GN artificial network with 128 nodes.

between the number of nodes and number of edges in the same community. Figure 3.8 shows an artificial network with 5 communities generated by LFR. Compared with GN artificial network, in this network, number of nodes in each community is different and the node degree follows power-law distribution; therefore, it better conforms to topological structure characteristics of real networks. To simulate the characteristics of overlapping community structure in real networks, users can also set the number of overlapping nodes in LFR artificial networks to provide communities with overlapping structure for detection algorithms. Based on

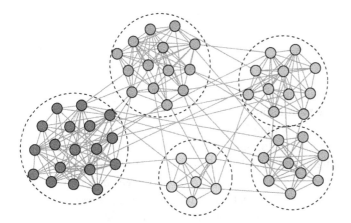

Figure 3.8: LFR artificial networks with 5 communities.

the above features, many scholars have used LFR artificial network to simulate online social networks of large scale and have evaluated various property indexes of virtual community detection algorithms in online social networks.

3.3 Static calculation detection algorithms for virtual communities

The existing network community detection algorithms can be classified into many classes based on different standards. For example, overlapping community detection algorithms and non-overlapping community detection algorithms based on whether the detected communities overlap; network topology-based algorithms, network dynamics-based algorithms, modularity function optimization-based algorithms and other algorithms based on different physical background; static calculation algorithms and dynamic calculation algorithms based on different calculation mechanism. For static calculation, each calculation step considers all nodes in the network and calculates whether certain partitioning conforms to global optimization objectives, thus. determines the final community structure. For dynamic calculation, starting from local nodes, update local node status according to certain rules and gradually infer the final global partitioning results of all nodes, while intermediary steps do not need to meet the global optimization objective of all nodes. Static calculation detection algorithms are introduced in this section and dynamic calculation algorithms will be introduced in the next section.

3.3.1 Modularity optimization algorithms

As mentioned above, Mark Newman proposed the concept of modularity to measure the intensity of community structure and is defined as (see Section 3.2.3)

$$Q = \frac{1}{2m} \sum_{ij} \left[A_{ij} - \frac{k_i k_i}{2m} \right] \delta(C_i, C_j) \tag{3.7}$$

The modularity value mainly depends on community partitioning of nodes in network C, i.e., the community partitioning situation in network, which can quantitatively measure the quality of community partitioning. Higher modularity value indicates better partitioning. Thus, optimal community partitioning of networks can be achieved by maximizing the modularity Q. The number of possible partitioning of a network is enormous. If the number of nodes and edges of a network are respectively denoted as n and m, the number of possible partitioning is exponent of n. Thus it is a NP-hard problem to find out optimal partition among all possible partitions. Some algorithms have been proposed to detect approximate optimal partition maximizing the modularity in reasonable time. Some of them are introduced below.

1. Classic Greedy algorithm

Mark Newman proposed a greedy modularity optimization algorithm FN [1]. Greedy algorithm aims to find overall optimal value or approximate optimal value of objective function. It decomposes entire optimization problem into multiple local optimization problems and find out optimal values of all local optimization problems which are integrated into overall approximate optimal value. In this sense, FN decomposes modularity optimization problem into local modularity optimization problems. First, regard each node of network as a small independent community; second, calculate the modularity gain of merging each two connected communities. Two communities whose combination leads to largest modularity gain or smallest modularity loss are selected to merging into a new community according to greedy principle. Repeat the iteration until all nodes are grouped into one community. The modularity values are changing along with the iteration and the community partition corresponding to largest modularity value is regarded as the approximate optimal one.

The specific steps of greedy algorithm FN are described below.

(1) Remove all edges in the network and regard each node of a network as an independent community.

(2) Regard each connected part as a community in the network and add edges out of the network back to the network, one edge at a time. If the added edge connects two different communities, merge them and calculate the modularity increment of the newly-formed community. Choose the two connected communities resulting in the greatest increase (or smallest decrease) in modularity for merging.

(3) If the number of communities is larger than 1, return to step (2), otherwise go to step (4).

(4) Select the partition with largest modularity among all iterations as the optimal community partition for the network.

In this algorithm, it should be noted that newly-added edge only affect the community partitioning of the network, and each calculation of modularity of network partitioning is completed on the intact topological structure of the network, i.e., the network including all edges in the network.

The FN algorithm is further illustrated based on Figure 3.2 below for better understanding of this algorithm.

(1) Initially, Remove all edges in the network and regard each node as an independent community, 9 communities totally.

(2) Add edges out of the network back to the network and calculate the modularity increment of the new community partition. The largest increase of modularity is

obtained when merging {8, 9} at $\Delta Q = 0.064$. Thus community {8} and {9} are firstly merged into community {8, 9}.

(3) Repeat step (2) for updated eight communities until all nodes are grouped into one community. There are nine different community partitions along with the iterations with the tree diagram of communities partitioned by FN shown in Figure 3.9.

(4) The community structure with largest modularity value is obtained when network is partitioned by dash line in Figure 3.9. The largest modularity value is $Q = 0.36$ and the resulted community structure contains two communities, i.e., {1,2,3,4} and {5,6,7,8,9}.

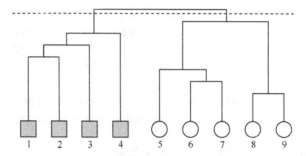

Figure 3.9: Dendrogram of communities partitioned by FN algorithm on example network.

The calculation performance of this algorithm is as follows. Assume that the network has n nodes and m edges. There are $n - 1$ iterations in FN. Since one pair of communities is merged in each iteration, $n - 1$ join operations are carried out entirely to construct the complete dendrogram. In each join, at most m possible pairs of communities need to be checked in time $O(m)$, and joining two communities takes $O(n)$ to update the adjacency matrix of network. Thus, the total time complexity of FN is $O((m + n)n)$, which is approximate to $O(n^2)$ in sparse networks. Though Mark Newman used this algorithm to analyze a co-authorship network with 56,276 nodes successfully, the time complexity of FN is still large. FN is only suitable to detect community structures in small social networks.

There are other heuristic algorithms for obtaining optimal modularity like simulated annealing algorithm [15], extremum optimization algorithm [16], etc. Simulated annealing algorithm obtains optimal modularity value more close to real maximum but requires larger time complexity. Extremum optimization algorithm obtains slightly worse modularity but much better time complexity.

2. Fast modularity optimization algorithm

To reduce time complexity, Blondel et al. proposed a hierarchical greedy algorithm [17] which includes two labels. In the first stage, regard each node as a community and decide the neighbor communities to be merged based on maximized modularity increment. The second stage begins after a round of scanning. All communities resulting from the first stage are regarded as nodes to construct a new network. Repeat the first stage in the new network. Repeat the two labels alternatively until the modularity value ceases to increase and obtain the approximate optimal community partition of a network.

This algorithm has some advantages. First, the algorithm is intuitive and easy to implement. Second, the number of communities does not need to be set in advance. Third, it can present the hierarchical virtual community structures of an online social network and detect community structures in different resolutions. Finally, simulation experiments show that the algorithm has nearly linear time complexity in sparse networks. It can partition the network with more than 10^9 nodes in reasonable time. Thus, this algorithm is suitable for detecting community structures in online social networks, a kind of complex network with super-large-scale.

3.3.2 Multi-objective optimization algorithms

Optimization algorithms represented by modularity optimization algorithm convert the virtual community detection problem to the extremum optimization problem, thereby solving the problem by heuristic algorithms such as simulated annealing algorithms. Online social networks are abstraction of real social networks, wherein communities usually have several kinds of characteristics in structures and properties and are difficult to be described by a single characteristic. To solve this problem, many scholars detect virtual community structures in online social networks by adopting multi-objective optimization theory based on traditional modularity optimization algorithms. Several multi-objective optimization algorithms are given below.

1. Community detection algorithms based on cellular automata

As mentioned above, traditional community detection algorithms based on modularity have many defects. For example, recent research showed that a community would be partitioned into large adjacent community through community detection algorithms based on modularity when the scale of community structure is too small. In this case, the value of modularity is big but the partition may be unreasonable. Moreover, communities in online social networks usually have several kinds of characteristics in structure and properties and are difficult to be described by a single characteristic. To solve this problem, many scholars have described the community structure in different aspects by adopting multi-objective optimization theory and partitioned virtual community structures by heuristic algorithms, such as cellular automata principle and genetic algorithms.

Yuxin Zhao proposed a CLA-net algorithm based on cellular learning automata in which each node is regarded as a learning automata based on irregular cellular automata [18]. Each learning automata describes the community structure regarding the community structure of the entire network and local community structure of nodes. Irregular cellular automata refers to the biological breeding phenomenon and creates a local dynamic model with discrete time dimension and space dimension. This model is not compliant with strict mathematical equations or function, but develops some simple rules by repeated computations based on the definitions of changing rules of cellular states for generating an extremely complex dynamic model. Zhao et al. mapped the online social network as irregular cellular learning automata and adjusted the state of each node dynamically to make the community structure more reasonable by customized evolution rules.

To introduce the algorithm specifically, some variants of learning automata L_i for each node i are defined as follows: α_i denotes the behavior aggregate of learning automata L_i and each alternative behavior corresponds to the sequence number of an adjacent node of node i; p_i denotes the behavior probability vector of learning automata L_i and p_{ij} denotes the probability of behavior j; $\alpha_i(t)$ denotes the behavior that L_i selects in the tth iteration; $\beta_i(t)$ is the feedback signal accepted by L_i in the tth iteration and $\beta_i(t) = 0$ denotes the reward signal while $\beta_i(t) = 1$ denotes the punishment signal. $W_{ij}(t)$ denotes times of the reward behavior j in the tth iteration; $Z_{ij}(t)$ denotes times of behavior j in the tth iteration; Q_{best} denotes the optimum value of modularity in current community structure.

The learning and updating process of learning automata L_i is described below.

(1) Choose a behavior $\alpha_i(t)$ randomly according to the behavior probability vector p_i.
(2) Interact with local environment (other adjacent nodes) and overall environment (the entire network), then obtain the feedback signal $\beta_i(t)$. If node i belongs to the same community as its most adjacent nodes and the modularity obtained in this iteration satisfies the inequality $Q(t) \geq Q_{best}$. Then the feedback signal $\beta_i(t) = 0$, otherwise $\beta_i(t) = 1$.
(3) Assume $\alpha_i(t) = \alpha_{iq}$ and update $W_{iq}(t)$ and $Z_{iq}(t)$ according to the feedback signal $\beta_i(t)$.

$$\begin{cases} W_{iq}(t) = W_{iq}(t-1) + (1 - \beta_i(t)) \\ Z_{iq}(t) = Z_{iq}(t-1) + 1 \end{cases} \tag{3.8}$$

(4) Update the optimum behavior of learning automata L_i according to the formula below and the optimum behavior refers to the one with the maximum value of $D_{ij}(t)$.

$$D_{ij}(t) = \frac{W_{ij}(t)}{Z_{ij}(t)} \tag{3.9}$$

(5) Assume the optimum behavior is α_{im} and update current learning automata L_i according to the behavior probability vector p_i, where a denotes the award coefficient and p_j denotes the jth component of vector p_i.

$$p_j(t+1) = \begin{cases} p_j(t) + a(1 - p_j(t)) & j = m \\ (1 - a)p_j(t) & j \neq m \end{cases} \tag{3.10}$$

The procedure of the algorithm is described as below in detail:

(1) Initialize the learning automata of each node randomly.

(2) Each learning automata in the network select its own behavior according to self-behavior probability vector p_i and obtain the community structure after decoding.

(3) Every learning automata in the network learns and updates by interacting with local environment and overall environment.

(4) Repeat step 2 until the community structure is stable.

Essentially, CLA-net algorithm is a multi-objective optimization algorithm with modularity function as its objective function and the condition that $k_i(c_i(t)) \geq k_i(c')$ where $c_i(t)$ denotes the community number which the node belongs to and $k_i(C) = \sum_{j \in C} A_{ij}$. A is the adjacent matrix of the network.

Apply the algorithm to the example in Figure 3.2 and detect community in the following procedure:

In the initial stage of algorithm, the state-transition matrix P can be calculated according to the adjacent matrix, where each element is the reciprocal of node degree.

$$P = \begin{pmatrix} 0 & 1/3 & 1/3 & 1/3 & 0 & 0 & 0 & 0 & 0 \\ 1/3 & 0 & 1/3 & 1/3 & 0 & 0 & 0 & 0 & 0 \\ 1/4 & 1/4 & 0 & 1/4 & 1/4 & 0 & 0 & 0 & 0 \\ 1/4 & 1/4 & 1/4 & 0 & 1/4 & 0 & 0 & 0 & 0 \\ 0 & 0 & 1/4 & 1/4 & 0 & 1/4 & 1/4 & 0 & 0 \\ 0 & 0 & 0 & 0 & 1/3 & 0 & 1/3 & 1/3 & 0 \\ 0 & 0 & 0 & 0 & 1/3 & 1/3 & 0 & 1/3 & 0 \\ 0 & 0 & 0 & 0 & 0 & 1/3 & 1/3 & 0 & 1/3 \\ 0 & 0 & 0 & 0 & 0 & 0 & 0 & 1 & 0 \end{pmatrix}$$

The award matrix W and selection matrix Z are as follows:

$$W = \begin{pmatrix} 0 & 3 & 4 & 0 & 0 & 0 & 0 & 0 & 0 \\ 5 & 0 & 1 & 1 & 0 & 0 & 0 & 0 & 0 \\ 3 & 4 & 0 & 0 & 0 & 0 & 0 & 0 & 0 \\ 1 & 3 & 3 & 0 & 0 & 0 & 0 & 0 & 0 \\ 0 & 0 & 0 & 0 & 0 & 5 & 1 & 0 & 0 \\ 0 & 0 & 0 & 0 & 4 & 0 & 0 & 2 & 0 \\ 0 & 0 & 0 & 0 & 2 & 2 & 0 & 2 & 0 \\ 0 & 0 & 0 & 0 & 0 & 3 & 3 & 0 & 1 \\ 0 & 0 & 0 & 0 & 0 & 0 & 0 & 7 & 0 \end{pmatrix},$$

$$Z = \begin{pmatrix} 0 & 16 & 21 & 13 & 0 & 0 & 0 & 0 & 0 \\ 18 & 0 & 16 & 16 & 0 & 0 & 0 & 0 & 0 \\ 13 & 15 & 0 & 10 & 12 & 0 & 0 & 0 & 0 \\ 16 & 11 & 13 & 0 & 10 & 0 & 0 & 0 & 0 \\ 0 & 0 & 16 & 13 & 0 & 13 & 8 & 0 & 0 \\ 0 & 0 & 0 & 0 & 14 & 0 & 13 & 23 & 0 \\ 0 & 0 & 0 & 0 & 19 & 11 & 0 & 20 & 0 \\ 0 & 0 & 0 & 0 & 0 & 17 & 14 & 0 & 19 \\ 0 & 0 & 0 & 0 & 0 & 0 & 0 & 50 & 0 \end{pmatrix}$$

Calculate the value of matrix D according to matrix W and Z and let $D_i(t) = W_i(t)/Z_i(t)$. The optimum Q_{best} of community structure after the initialization is 0.3571.

The partition of community structure after an iteration is shown in Table 3.1.

As shown above, node 1 and node 4 belong to the same community; node 2 and node 4 belong to the same community; node 3 and node 1 belong to the same community; node 4 and node 1 belong to the same community, and so on. The partition of the community is shown in Table 3.2 after decoding.

Table 3.1: The partition of community structure after an iteration.

Node number	1	2	3	4	5	6	7	8	9
Adjacent node	4	4	1	1	6	7	8	6	8

Table 3.2: The partition of the community after decoding.

Node number	1	2	3	4	5	6	7	8	9
Community number	1	1	1	1	2	2	2	2	2

The value of Q_{best} is 0.3571. All nodes are awarded because the value of Q_{best} remains the same and each node satisfies the condition $k_i(c_i(t)) \geq k_i(c')$. According to Formula 3.8, the award matrix W and selection matrix Z updated are as below.

$$W = \begin{pmatrix} 0 & 3 & 4 & 1 & 0 & 0 & 0 & 0 & 0 \\ 5 & 0 & 1 & 2 & 0 & 0 & 0 & 0 & 0 \\ 4 & 4 & 0 & 0 & 0 & 0 & 0 & 0 & 0 \\ 2 & 3 & 3 & 0 & 0 & 0 & 0 & 0 & 0 \\ 0 & 0 & 0 & 0 & 0 & 6 & 1 & 0 & 0 \\ 0 & 0 & 0 & 0 & 4 & 0 & 1 & 2 & 0 \\ 0 & 0 & 0 & 0 & 2 & 2 & 0 & 3 & 0 \\ 0 & 0 & 0 & 0 & 0 & 4 & 3 & 0 & 1 \\ 0 & 0 & 0 & 0 & 0 & 0 & 0 & 8 & 0 \end{pmatrix},$$

$$Z = \begin{pmatrix} 0 & 16 & 21 & 14 & 0 & 0 & 0 & 0 & 0 \\ 18 & 0 & 16 & 17 & 0 & 0 & 0 & 0 & 0 \\ 14 & 15 & 0 & 10 & 12 & 0 & 0 & 0 & 0 \\ 17 & 11 & 13 & 0 & 10 & 0 & 0 & 0 & 0 \\ 0 & 0 & 16 & 13 & 0 & 14 & 8 & 0 & 0 \\ 0 & 0 & 0 & 0 & 14 & 0 & 14 & 23 & 0 \\ 0 & 0 & 0 & 0 & 19 & 11 & 0 & 21 & 0 \\ 0 & 0 & 0 & 0 & 0 & 18 & 14 & 0 & 19 \\ 0 & 0 & 0 & 0 & 0 & 0 & 0 & 51 & 0 \end{pmatrix}$$

Then update matrix D according to the formula $D_i(t) = W_i(t)/Z_i(t)$. According to Formula 3.10, the updated state-transition matrix P is shown as below.

$$P = \begin{pmatrix} 0 & 0.2667 & 0.4666 & 0.2667 & 0 & 0 & 0 & 0 & 0 \\ 0.4666 & 0 & 0.2667 & 0.2667 & 0 & 0 & 0 & 0 & 0 \\ 0.4 & 0.2 & 0 & 0.2 & 0.2 & 0 & 0 & 0 & 0 \\ 0.2 & 0.4 & 0.2 & 0 & 0.2 & 0 & 0 & 0 & 0 \\ 0 & 0 & 0.2 & 0.2 & 0 & 0.4 & 0.2 & 0 & 0 \\ 0 & 0 & 0 & 0 & 0.4666 & 0 & 0.2667 & 0.2667 & 0 \\ 0 & 0 & 0 & 0 & 0.2667 & 0.4666 & 0 & 0.2667 & 0 \\ 0 & 0 & 0 & 0 & 0 & 0.4666 & 0.2667 & 0 & 0.2667 \\ 0 & 0 & 0 & 0 & 0 & 0 & 0 & 1 & 0 \end{pmatrix}$$

The results after several times of iteration is shown in Table 3.3.

Table 3.3: The community partition after several times of iteration.

Node number	1	2	3	4	5	6	7	8	9
Community number	1	1	1	1	2	2	2	2	2

2. Multi-objective optimization algorithms on overlapping structure

The virtual community structure in online social networks is diverse, in which the overlapping community structure is a typical example. To detect virtual communities with overlapping structure in online networks, Du et al. extended the existing multi-objective optimization algorithms to the field of overlapping community structure detection [19]. In the algorithm, the topological structure of network is coded as gene sequence by edge-based mapping pattern to denotes the situation that the same node belongs to several communities through edge clustering in network. The algorithm regards the partition density function (Formula 3.11) and the modularity function (Formula 3.11) in overlapping communities proposed by Shen et al. as objective function, which is defined as:

$$D = \frac{2}{M} \sum_c m_c \frac{m_c - (n_c - 1)}{(n_c - 2)(n_c - 1)} \tag{3.11}$$

$$Q_{OL} = \frac{1}{2m} \sum_{k=1}^{c} \sum_{i,j \in C_k} \frac{1}{O_i O_j} \left[A_{ij} - \frac{k_i k_j}{2m} \right] \tag{3.12}$$

The topological structure of network is coded as gene sequence based on adjacency of edge tracks. In addition, the gene sequence can be optimized by genetic algorithms. Simulation results show that the algorithm can accurately detect the community structure in complex networks.

3.3.3 Algorithms based on probability model

Bayesian probability model is widely used in topic detection initially [24] and has been applied in community detection algorithms. Probability model-based algorithms infer network model by maximizing Bayesian likelihood probability to obtain real network partition. The network model defines clustering structure by assuming the connection pattern among nodes and infer the best fit model to the observed network by maximizing Bayesian likelihood probability, thus obtaining the community structure. Some community detection algorithms based on probability model are introduced below.

1. Algorithms based on mixed model

Newman et al. proposed a community detection algorithm in directed networks based on mixed model and expectation-maximization strategy. Given a directed network G with adjacency matrix A, its n nodes are partitioned into c communities. The mixed model parameters of such network is defined as follows.

g_i: the community of node i;

π_r: the ratio between number of nodes in community r and number of nodes in network;

θ_{ri}: the probability that a directed edge from a certain node in community r to node i;

According to definition, the sets $\{\pi_r\}$ and $\{\theta_{ri}\}$ satisfy the normalization condition:

$$\sum_{r=1}^{c} \pi_r = 1, \quad \sum_{i=1}^{n} \theta_{ri} = 1 \tag{3.13}$$

The algorithm calculates the optimal value of parameters $\{\pi_r\}$ and $\{\theta_{ri}\}$ by fitting the mixed model to adjacency matrix A of observed network data.

According to defined parameters above, the connection probability between node i and j in mixed model is $p_{ij} = \pi_{g_i} \theta_{g_i, j}$.

The likelihood probability that the observed network is generated by mixed model with parameters $\{\pi_r\}$ and $\{\theta_{ri}\}$ is:

$$P(A, g|\pi, \theta) = P(A|g, \pi, \theta)P(g|\pi, \theta) \tag{3.14}$$

where

$$P(A|g, \pi, \theta) = \Pi_{ij}\theta_{g_i, j}^{A_{ij}}, \, P(g|\pi, \theta) = \Pi_i\pi_{g_i} \tag{3.15}$$

So the likelihood probability is:

$$P(A, g|, \pi, \theta) = \Pi_i\pi_{g_i}\Pi_{ij}\theta_{g_i, j}^{A_{ij}}$$

So the logarithm of likelihood probability $P(A, g|\pi, \theta)$ is:

$$L = \ln P(A, g|\pi, \theta) = \sum_i \left[\ln\pi_{g_i} + \sum_j A_{ij}\ln\theta_{g_i, j} \right] \tag{3.16}$$

The logarithm of likelihood probability is the objective function of the algorithm. The algorithm calculates the optimal value of parameters $\{\pi_r\}$ and $\{\theta_{ri}\}$ by maximizing the likelihood probability to determine the mixed model best fit to the observed network data. However, another unknown parameter g_i needs to be handled in the mixed model. For this purpose, a new parameter denoting the probability of node i in community r is defined as:

$$q_{ir} = P(g_i = r|A, \pi, \theta) = \frac{\pi_r\Pi_j\theta_{rj}^{A_{ij}}}{\sum_s \pi_s\Pi_j\theta_{sj}^{A_{ij}}} \tag{3.17}$$

The expected value $\bar{L}$ for the log-likelihood based on q_{ir} is calculated as

$$\bar{L} = \sum_{ir} q_{ir} \left[\ln\pi_r + \sum_j A_{ij}\ln\theta_{rj} \right] \tag{3.18}$$

The parameters $\{\pi_r\}$ and $\{\theta_{ri}\}$ can be determined by maximizing expected value L under the normalization condition of $\{\pi_r\}$ and $\{\theta_{ri}\}$, i.e.,

$$\pi_r = \frac{1}{n}\sum_i q_{ir}, \, \theta_{rj} = \frac{\sum_i A_{ij}q_{ir}}{\sum_i k_i q_{ir}} \tag{3.19}$$

where k_i is the out degree of node i. The final value of parameters $\{\pi_r\}$, $\{\theta_{ri}\}$ and $\{q_{ir}\}$ can be calculated by applying EM algorithm on Formula 3.17 and Formula 3.19. The steps of this algorithm are described below.

Input: the number of communities in network c, the maximal iteration number of algorithm maxiter.

(1) Initially, iteration number is set as $t = 0$, and initial value of parameters $\{\pi_r\}_0$ and $\{\theta_{ri}\}_0$ are set as random values satisfying the normalization condition (3.13).

(2) Update values of parameter $\{q_{ir}\}_t$ by substituting current values of parameters $\{\pi_r\}_t$ and $\{\theta_{ri}\}_t$ into equation (3.17).

(3) Update values of parameters $\{\pi_r\}_{t+1}$ and $\{\theta_{ri}\}_{t+1}$ by substituting current values of parameter $\{q_{ir}\}_t$ into equation (3.19).

(4) Update iteration number as $t = t + 1$. If $t > maxiter$, output the values of $\{q_{ir}\}_t$ and terminate the algorithm, otherwise go to step (5).

(5) Calculate the difference between values of parameter q in latest two iterations, i.e., $\Delta q = \|q_t - q_{t-1}\|$. If $\Delta q = 0$ which means the value of parameter q converges, end the algorithm and output the values of q, otherwise return to step (2) and continue iterations.

Note that the initial values of parameters π and θ should avoid unstable point of Formula 3.17 and Formula 3.19, i.e., $\pi_i = \frac{1}{c}$, $\theta_{ri} = \frac{1}{n}$.

The algorithm can be extended to deal with undirected networks naturally. In undirected network cases, the parameter θ_{ri} is defined as the connection probability between nodes in community r and node i. Other derivation processes are the same as those in directed network cases and finally obtain results of community portioning by Formula 3.17 and Formula 3.19. The outputting probability q_{ir} can be regarded as the belongingness intensity of node i in community r. One disadvantage of such algorithm is that the number of communities c needs to be set in advance while such number is usually unknown.

Newman et al. evaluate the algorithm in social network of U.S. high school students. The obtained community structure is illustrated in Figure 3.10. As shown in Figure 3.10, the algorithm partitioned the network into two communities, one of which mainly contains most black students in school and the other one mainly includes most white students. Students in other races uniformly belong to two communities, i.e., community structure of high school has strong relation to races of students.

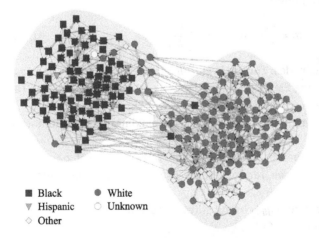

■ Black   ● White
▼ Hispanic   ○ Unknown
◇ Other

Figure 3.10: Social network of U.S. high school students from Newman M [22].

2. Edge-based mixed model algorithm

Ren et al. propose another mixed model based on edges to handle undirected networks. Given a undirected network G whose adjacency matrix is A, its n nodes are partitioned into c communities. The neighbor node set of a node i is denoted as $N(i)$. Similarly, the fraction of nodes in community r is π_r. Suppose that the probability that community r selects node i is β_{ri} which satisfies normalization condition $\sum_{r=1}^{c} \beta_{ri} = 1$. Larger value of β_{ri} indicates more importance of the node i in community r. Note that the node i can be selected by multiple communities. Assume that communities select different nodes independently, then the probability that the mixed model generates edge e_{ij} is:

$$P(e_{ij}|\pi, \beta) = \sum_{r=1}^{c} \pi_r \beta_{ri} \beta_{rj} \tag{3.20}$$

The log-likelihood probability that such model generates all edges in network is:

$$L = \ln P(A|\pi, \beta) = \sum_{i=1}^{n} \sum_{j:j \in N(i)} \ln \left(\sum_{r=1}^{c} \pi_r \beta_{ri} \beta_{rj} \right) \tag{3.21}$$

Similarly, the log-likelihood probability can be maximized by EM algorithm. Belongingness intensity of each edge to different communities are obtained by maximizing log-likelihood probability and belongingness intensity of each node to different communities are derived accordingly.

3. Algorithm based on LDA

LDA is a model for generating document topic and is also called three layer Bayesian probability model. LDA was first used to construct the three-layer model of word, topic and document [24], Yu et al. extend LDA model to overlapping community detection tasks [25] and propose an overlapping community detection algorithm LBLP based on LDA model. The algorithm includes three parts: network coding, edge LDA modeling, and model inference. The time complexity of algorithm is relatively low, making it suitable for large online social network analysis.

3.3.4 Information coding algorithms

To compress the topology information, researchers introduced the idea of information coding in information theory and thereby designed new community detection algorithms. In information theory, information coding methods compress original information capacity by encoding more information with less codes according to the minimum description length (MDL) principle. The main idea of the MDL principle is that any rules in data can be used to compress data. The cohesive virtual community structure is an important law of data in online social networks. As a result, virtual community structure in online social network can be used to describe the information flow in network through compressive coding. Several algorithms are introduced as below.

1. Infomap algorithm

Rosvall et al. proposed the Infomap algorithm based on the information theory [5]. The algorithm uses random-walking as the agency of information spreading in network which will generate corresponding data flow. The amount of information generated by random-walking can be measured by the length of code in each step of random-walking, which is the average length of codes. Effective coding algorithms are needed for compressing the average length of codes up to the hilt. Huffman coding is a common coding algorithm which distributes short codes to each node visited by random-walking. Apply the Huffman coding to Figure 3.2 and the results as is shown in Figure 3.11. The information source coding theory of Shannon provides the theoretical boundary for the code length of Huffman coding: the average code length in every step should not be less than the entropy of variable X, i.e., $H(x) = - \sum_1^n p_i \log(p_i)$. The sample space of variable X is set of nodes and the probability distribution of X is the visiting frequency of each node by random-walking. As Huffman coding doesn't use the regularity of network structure, the average length of codes is still large. The second level coding underlining community structure can be considered to further compress the length of information flow.

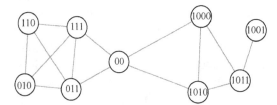

Figure 3.11: Coding on the example only by Huffman coding.

Second-level coding on the network in Figure 3.2, which is shown in Figure 3.12, allocates a unique codeword for each community in the network and different codewords for all the nodes in the same community. Codewords can be reused for nodes in different communities. This rule is similar to the naming rule on the map. Communities are similar to cities and nodes to streets in a city. Streets in different cities can share the same name while different streets in the same city cannot share the same name. Compared with the coding in Figure 3.11, this rule can be used to effectively reduce the length of codeword. The access frequency of communities or nodes can also be regarded as the probability distribution of variables, with

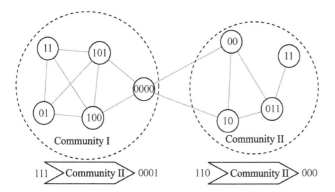

Figure 3.12: Second level coding on the example.

codewords of communities and the nodes inside coded by Huffman coding. A leave code for previous community and a codeword for the community behind are needed in description in each random-walking between different communities to denote differences in communities. Second-level coding algorithm converts the community partition problem to the problem of optimum coding, i.e., finding an optimum partition with minimal average description length in random-walking. The description length includes the codeword length in random-walking in communities and between communities. Obviously, better community partition leads to lower shifting frequency between communities, reducing the average codeword length of communities. Moreover, the codeword length of node is greatly reduced because of the second-level coding, resulting in significant compression of the overall length of description. On the contrary, the shifting will be more frequent and the length of random-walking description cannot be compressed if the communities are not partitioned well.

Assume a community partition of given network with n nodes in the network partitioned into m communities. Then, the average description length $L(M)$ in every step of random-walking is expressed in the equation below.

$$L(M) = q_\frown H(Q) + \sum_{i=1}^{m} p_\circlearrowleft^i H(p^i) \tag{3.22}$$

Formula 3.22 is called map equation, where $q_{\textrm{D}}H(Q)$ denotes the average codeword length of shifting between communities and $\sum_{i=1}^{m} p_\circlearrowleft^i H(p^i)$ denotes the average codeword length in random-walking. The purpose of community detection in networks to find the optimal partition with the minimal average codeword length.

Use an algorithm similar to the greedy algorithm in Section 3.3.1 to detect optimal partition, i.e., allocate a community for each node at first and combine two communities which lead to the most reduction in average description length $L(M)$. Repeat this process until communities are merged into one. The steps of the algorithm in detail is shown below.

(1) Delete all edges in the network and regard each node as a community in the network.
(2) Consider each connected part as a community in the network and add edges outside the network back to the network. If the added edge connects two different communities, then combine these two communities. Calculate the decrement in average description length of the new partition and combine the two communities which lead to the most reduction in the average description length.
(3) If the number of communities is more than one, then return to step (2) for iteration, otherwise go to step (4).
(4) Choose the community partition with the minimal average description length as the optimal partition of network by traversing the values of average description length of different community partitions.

Apply the Infomap algorithm to the example in this chapter with detailed steps shown as below.
(1) Regard each node as a community in the network, 9 communities in total, and calculate the average description length $L(M) = 5.132$.
(2) Combine any two communities and calculate the average description length of new communities. It is found that the combination of community {8} and {9} leads to the most reduction in average description length $\Delta L(M) = -0.3393$. As a result, the first step is to combine community {8} and {9} to community {8, 9}.
(3) Continue the process above until communities are merged into one. There are 9 different partitions in this process. The community spanning tree generated by the algorithm is shown in Figure 3.13.

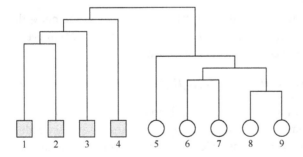

Figure 3.13: The community spanning tree generated by Informap algorithm on the example.

(4) Traverse the values of average description length in different community partitions. It is found that the average description length has the minimal value $L(M) = 3.100$ if the network is partitioned into two communities {1, 2, 3, 4} and {5, 6, 7, 8, 9}, which is the optimal partition of the network.

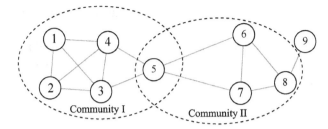

Figure 3.14: The overlapping community structure of example detected by CPM algorithm.

The Infomap algorithm detects the communities by the rule of information propagation in network. The algorithm is better than modularity optimization algorithm when the difference in size of communities is large. As the size of virtual communities in online social network is always different, Infomap algorithm is more accurate than modularity optimization algorithm.

2. The map equation of edge community

Original Infomap algorithm can only detect nonoverlapping communities while online social networks usually have overlapping community structure. As a result, Kim et al. extended the map equation to detect edge communities in networks [26]. Different from node communities, edge communities are partitioned by edges which partitions edges in networks into non-overlapping communities. The community of a node depends on its connected edge. As a node can be connected to several edges at the same time. A node will be partitioned into different communities if its connected edges are partitioned into different communities, forming the overlapping community structure. Kim et al. extended the map equation to detect edge communities in networks by modifying the coding rule of random-walking. The first level codes are allocated to edge communities in the network whereas the second level codes are allocated to nodes, and nodes belonging to different communities are allocated with different second level codes. As a result, the number of second level codes of each node is the same as the number of community which it belongs to. Random-walking will be still carried out on node and each step of random-walking starts from the source node to the target node going by an edge. If the edge in the current step is different from that in previous step, record code of the current community and the secondary code of the target node. If these two edges are the same, record the second level code of the target node only. The map equation of edge community is shown as below.

$$L_{\text{linkcom}}(M) = q_{\curvearrowright} H(Q) + \sum_{i=1}^{m} p^i_{\circlearrowleft} H(p^i) \qquad (3.23)$$

Formula 3.23 and formula 3.22 are the same in expression, but are different in partition M and probability distribution $q_\curvearrowleft$ and $p_\circlearrowleft^i$.

Although overlapping nodes have several second level codes which lead to redundancy, when the edge community partition is better than community partition of nodes, the utilization frequency of first level coding will be lowered along with the frequency reduction of random-walking between different communities. The reduction in average coding length can compensate for the redundancy of second level code. Moreover, Kim et al. thought that a network has important overlapping structure when the minimal description length $L_{linkcom}$ in edge community partition is smaller than that in community partition of nodes. Therefore, they defined an index to measure the overlapping degree of communities in online social networks: the significance of overlapping which is calculated below.

$$O = \frac{L_{\mathrm{nodecom}} - L_{\mathrm{linkcom}}}{L_{\mathrm{nodecom}} + L_{\mathrm{linkcom}}} \tag{3.24}$$

The value of the significance of overlapping satisfies the condition $O \in (-1, 1)$. The overlapping structure is obvious if the value is positive.

Kim et al. analyzed the blog network of U.S. politicians by map equation which has 1,490 nodes and 19,090 edges [27]. By applying the map equation to node communities and edge communities respectively, they obtained the minimal description length in node communities of $L_{\mathrm{nodecom}} = 8.93$ and that in edge communities of $L_{\mathrm{linkcom}} = 8.65$. Moreover, the significance of overlapping of the network is $O = 0.0163$, which shows that online social networks, such as the Blog network, have obvious overlapping community structure.

3. Fast algorithm by minimizing the map equation

Fast algorithm to minimize the map equation is needed for online social networks of large scale. Rosvall et al. proposed the fast algorithm by minimizing the map equation [28] according to the fast modularity optimization algorithm [17]. The core of this algorithm is divided into two labels. In the first stage, partition all nodes into independent communities and scan these communities randomly to combine the communities according to the largest reduction principle of map equation. Then start second stage after a round of scanning and reconstruct the network by regarding the communities obtained in first stage as new nodes in the network. Repeat these two labels alternatively until the value of map equation cannot be reduced any more.

Jin et al. proposed the community detection algorithm InfoMR [29] based on MapReduce parallel framework by combining the information compression coding algorithm and parallel computation. The algorithm has low complexity and is suitable for online social networks of large scale because of the parallel computation mechanism.

3.4 Dynamic calculation detection algorithms for virtual communities

3.4.1 Clique percolation algorithms

In online social networks, users can usually take part in different groups and topics, leading to an overlapping virtual community structure. The detection problem of overlapping communities is first proposed by Palla et al. [6]. To solve this problem, some clique percolation algorithms are proposed considering that a node can belong to different cliques. Some clique percolation algorithms are introduced as below.

1. CPM algorithm
Cliques refer to complete subgraphs in networks which can also be called as groups. A subgraph with k nodes can be defined as $k-$clique [6]. Internal edges of communities easily form clique due to high density of edges in the community and low density of edges between communities. Based on the characteristic above, Palla et al. proposed the CPM algorithm [6]. Some basic concepts are introduced as below.
(1) Adjacent $k-$clique: two $k-$cliques are adjacent if they share $k-1$ nodes with each other.
(2) $k-$clique chain: a set of a series of continuous $k-$cliques is defined as a $k-$clique chain.
(3) The connectivity of $k-$clique: if two $k-$cliques are parts of the same $k-$clique chain, they can be deemed as connected.
(4) $k-$clique community: connected $k-$cliques in network, i.e., the set of all $k-$cliques which connect with each other by a series of adjacent k cliques.

These concepts above can be explained with Figure 3.2 in this chapter. Assume $k=3$, $3-$cliques in example include $\{1, 2, 3\}$, $\{1, 3, 4\}$, $\{3, 4, 5\}$, etc. Among all $3-$cliques, $\{1, 2, 3\}$ and $\{1, 3, 4\}$ are adjacent because they share node 1 and node 3. $\{1, 2, 3\}$, $\{1, 3, 4\}$ and $\{3, 4, 5\}$ form a $3-$clique chain in which $\{1, 2, 3\}$ and $\{3, 4, 5\}$ are $3-$clique connected. At last, the set $\{1, 2, 3, 4, 5\}$ forms a $3-$clique connected part called as a $3-$clique community. According to the steps above, another $3-$clique community in example is $\{5, 6, 7, 8\}$. As shown in figure, the communities partitioned are overlapped as these two $3-$clique communities include node 5 at the same time.. If k equals 4 in this example, the $4-$clique community is $\{1, 2, 3, 4\}$. Obviously, if the value of k is larger, the size of $k-$clique community will be smaller but the communities will be more cohesive.

Parameter k is a threshold value for complete subgraphs. In fact, complete subgraph with size s larger than k may exist. Obviously, a complete subgraph with size s will include C_s^k different $k-$cliques and they are $k-$cliques connected. If two large complete subgraphs share at least $k-1$ nodes, they are also $k-$clique connected and form a k-clique community. In the example, set {1, 2, 3, 4} is a 4-clique which includes four 3-cliques which are 3-clique connected. This 4-clique share two nodes with the 3-clique {3, 4, 5}. Thus, they are 3-clique connected and form a 3-clique community. To describe the algorithm simply, the cliques not belonging to other complete subgraphs will be called as the maximum clique. CPM algorithm detects overlapping communities by seeking the maximum cliques in networks of which the size is not smaller than k.

The steps of the algorithm is described as below.

Input: The threshold value for the size of clique is k.

(1) Find all the maximum cliques in the network.

(2) Construct the clique–clique overlapping matrix O. O is a symmetric matrix in $n_c \times n_c$ order. n_c denotes the number of maximum clique in the network. O_{ij} denotes the number of nodes shared by maximum clique i and j. O_{ii} denotes the size of the maximum clique.

(3) Nondiagonal elements smaller than $k-1$ and diagonal elements smaller than k are all set to 0, and the remaining elements are set to 1.

(4) Analyze the processed matrix O and find the connected part which is regarded as the final k-clique community.

Apply the algorithm to the example.

Input: The threshold value $k=3$.

(1) The maximum cliques in the network are {1, 2, 3, 4}, {3, 4, 5}, {5, 6, 7}, {6, 7, 8}, {8, 9}.

(2) Construct the clique–clique overlapping matrix of the network.

$$O = \begin{bmatrix} 4 & 2 & 0 & 0 & 0 \\ 2 & 3 & 1 & 0 & 0 \\ 0 & 1 & 3 & 2 & 0 \\ 0 & 0 & 2 & 3 & 1 \\ 0 & 0 & 0 & 1 & 2 \end{bmatrix}$$

(3) Nondiagonal elements smaller than 2 and diagonal elements smaller than 3 are set to 0, and the remaining elements are set to 1.

$$O = \begin{bmatrix} 1 & 1 & 0 & 0 & 0 \\ 1 & 1 & 0 & 0 & 0 \\ 0 & 0 & 1 & 1 & 0 \\ 0 & 0 & 1 & 1 & 0 \\ 0 & 0 & 0 & 0 & 0 \end{bmatrix}$$

(4) Analyze the processed matrix and find two connected part {1, 2, 3, 4, 5} and {5, 6, 7, 8}. These parts are two 3-cliques in the network with the overlapping node 5.

Detecting the maximum clique in the network is a NP complete problem. Palla et al. described an effective algorithm to detect the maximum clique in networks. First, specify the size s of the maximum clique according to the degree sequence of network nodes; second, select nodes repeatedly and extracts all the maximum cliques containing the node with size s; third, delete the nodes selected and their connected edges until there are no nodes left; at last, reduce the size by 1 and detect new maximum cliques in the network. Repeat this process until the size of the maximum clique is 0. The algorithm is fast in real networks because real networks are sparse and have limited maximum cliques.

In online social networks, users tend to form cliques. Large communities usually have many small groups in which users are related or close to each other and form the cliques in communities. At the same time, each user belongs to several groups and forms the overlapping structure in communities. Consiquently, detection algorithms on overlapping community structure based on cliques are suitable for community detection in online social networks.

2. CPMw algorithm

In terms of weighted online social networks, a standard algorithm is to set a threshold value for the edge weight. In this case, edges with weight less than the threshold value are excluded from the network and the remaining are regarded as unweighted edges which form a corresponding unweighted network. Finally, apply the CPMw algorithm on this unweighted network. Farkas et al. proposed another weighted clique percolation algorithm [30]. The authors defined the intensity of $k-$ clique according to the intensity of subgraph, where the intensity of a subgraph refers to the geometric average of all the weights of edges in the subgraph [31]. As a result, the intensity of $k-$ cliquecan be defined as follows:

$$I(C) = \left(\prod_{i<j; i, j \in C} w_{ij} \right)^{2/k(k-1)} \tag{3.25}$$

Different from basic algorithms, the algorithm sets a threshold for the intensity I. $k-$ clique with intensity larger than the threshold will be partitioned into the community; otherwise, it will be abandoned. Other steps in the algorithm is similar to CPM algorithm. The algorithm allows for edges with weight smaller than I in $k-$ cliques and considers the integrality of the topological structure in weighted online social networks, which avoids the situation that some users are partitioned into different communities by mistake because of their weak connection.

3. Fast clique percolation algorithms

Kumpula et al. proposed a fast clique percolation algorithm named SCP [32] for community detection in online social networks of large scale. The algorithm includes two stages. In the first stage, it aims to find $k-$ cliques in networks. Starting from an empty graph, the algorithm adds edges into the network one by one and inspects that if a new $k - clique$ is generated. In the second stage, regard the k – cliques generated above as input and judge whether k – cliques generated in first stage belongs to existing k – cliques by calculating the overlapping degree of them. A final partition will be generated by these two steps.

Time complexity of the algorithm is linear to the number of k – cliques and the run time is much shorter than that of the original CPM algorithm, especially in weighted networks. Original CPM algorithm needs to operate the algorithm for all the threshold values of weight, whereas SCP algorithm is operated only once, saving time. In terms of weighted social networks of large scale, the best threshold for the weight of relationship between users are uncertain, SCP algorithm can obtain overlapping community structure of all threshold values to find the best threshold value and best community structure.

3.4.2 Agglomerative algorithms based on similarity

In the real world, the community structure is usually organized in a hierarchical form. Take colleges as example, faculty and students can be partitioned into several communities according to their institutes. All members can also be partitioned into different departments while students in different classes of each department also form community structure. As abstraction and extension of real social relationship, online social networks are also organized in the hierarchical form. For example, on Facebook and other social networks, staff from the same company can form community structure as per their departments. While each community contains several subcommunities. Online social networks in China such as renren.com have similar hierarchical feature in community structure which has great importance in understanding the topological feature of the entire network and mining the function of each module in networks. For this purpose, many scholars design community detection algorithms to reveal the hierarchical community structure in topological structure of networks. Among these algorithms, agglomerative algorithms based on similarity are of great importance. They referred the idea of clustering in traditional pattern recognition. In the initial stage, regard each node as an independent community, and then merge two subcommunities with the biggest similarity into a bigger community until all nodes are merged into the biggest virtual community.

1. EAGLE algorithm

Virtual community aggregation algorithm based on similarity can easily detect a virtual community with a hierarchical structure and reveals structural characteristics of online social networks organized at different levels. Shen et al. proposed a typical hierarchical community aggregation algorithm, EAGLE algorithm [14], which detects all of the maximum clique with the technology of detecting the maximum clique. On this basis, use the traditional data clustering framework and iteratively merge sub-communities with the greatest similarity until the entire network is merged into a big community, where the degree of similarity between the sub-communities is expressed by the following formula:

$$M = \frac{1}{2m} \sum_{v \in C_1, w \in C_2, v \neq w} \left[A_{vw} - \frac{k_v k_w}{2m} \right] \qquad (3.26)$$

C_1 and C_2 denotes two communities, A_{vw} denotes the element of the network adjacency matrix, m denotes the number of edge in network diagram A, and k_v, k_w denotes the degree of node v and node w respectively.

Specific process is as follows:

(1) According to the network structure of the current input, detect the largest clique in the network with the Bron-Kerbosch algorithm; then filter the smallest scale clique according to a preset threshold k, and consider the maximum clique of the community with scale larger than k as initialized community structures, and calculate the similarity between communities using the Formula 3.26.

(2) Select two community structures which have maximum similarity and merge them into one community; then calculate the similarity of the new community and other communities.

(3) Repeat step (2) until the entire network merge into one large community structures.

(4) Determine the largest structure of the community partition which can make Formula 3.27 obtain the maximal value and output it as a result. Formula 3.27 is as follows:

$$EQ = \frac{1}{2m} \sum_i \sum_{v \in C_i, w \in C_i} \frac{1}{O_v O_w} \left[A_{vw} - \frac{k_v k_w}{2m} \right] \qquad (3.27)$$

O_v is the number of the community which node v belongs to. Community partition obtaining the largest EQ is the optimal partition of community structure.

The time complexity of EAGLE algorithm is as follows: For a network with n nodes, assume that the maximum number of clique is s in the initial state, h is the number of the maximum cliques sharing an edge, then step of the algorithm time complexity is $O(n^2)$ in step (1); in step (2), the merge of largest clique need to be operated $s - 1$ times. Every merge operation needs to partition $h + n$ communities and calculate similarity between new communities and other communities, so the time complexity is $O(h + n)$, therefore the first three steps of total time complexity is $O(n^2 + (h + n)s)$. According to Formula 3.27, the actual complexity of the step (4) is $O(n^2 s)$. Therefore, the real complexity is $O(n^2 + (h + n)s + n^2 s)$.

For example, detect the maximum clique in the network diagram by EAGLE algorithm in 3. Figure 3.2. There are four maximum cliques in the graph: {1, 2, 3, 4}, {3, 4, 5}, {5, 6, 7} and {6, 7, 8}. Based on the EAGLE algorithm, the isolated points except the maximum clique are also considered as a separate clique in the network, such as {9}. By Formula 3.26, we can calculate that the similarity between {5, 6, 7} and {6, 7, 8} as 0.0995. For all the neighboring maximum clique, it has the greatest similarity. Therefore, choose the biggest clique consolidation, merging {5, 6, 7} and {6, 7, 8} into the same community. After the second iteration, the similarity between the cliques {1, 2, 3, 4} and {3, 4, 5} is 0.0714, while the similarity between cliques {3, 4, 5,} and {5,6,7,8} is −0.0561. Therefore, in the second iteration, merge {1, 2, 3, 4} and {3, 4, 5} into {1, 2, 3, 4, 5}. In the third iteration, the similarity between cliques {5, 6, 7, 8} and {1, 2, 3, 4, 5} is −0.1556, while similarity between cliques {5, 6, 7, 8} and {9} is 0.0191, so merge clique {5, 6, 7, 8} and {9}. Finally, {1, 2, 3, 4, 5} and {5, 6, 7, 8, 9} are merged into one large clique. Clique merging tree is as shown in Figure 3.15. According to Formula 3.27, it is most reasonable when the community is partitioned in the position shown in dotted lines.

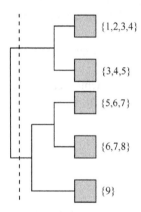

Figure 3.15: Clique merging tree in EAGLE algorithm.

2. Other agglomerative algorithms based on similarity

The most important part of aggregation algorithm based on the similarity is to calculate the similarity between the sub-communities. Using different similarity function has a certain influence on the final result of community partition. Over the past few decades, scholars in various fields have proposed various similarity formulas for this problem and depicted and measured the degree of similarity between different nodes from different perspectives. These similarity formulas mostly map sub-community structures to nodes in n-dimensional space, then measure the degree of similarity between these sub-communities by distance between nodes and other concepts. A typical concepts is the Euclidean distance, M distance, infinite norm and cosine similarity formula.

For two nodes $A = (a_1, a_2, \cdots, a_n)$ and $B = (b_1, b_2, \cdots, b_n)$, formulas based on the similarity of Euclidean distance, M distance and infinite norm are as follows:

$$d_{AB}^E = \sum_{k=1}^{n} \sqrt{(a_k - b_k)^2} \tag{3.28}$$

$$d_{AB}^M = \sum_{k=1}^{n} |a_k - b_k| \tag{3.29}$$

$$d_{AB}^\infty = \max_{k \in [1, n]} |a_k - b_k| \tag{3.30}$$

Experts and scholars of virtual community use the knowledge of geometry and statistics, then measure the similarity degree between communities based on cosine distance as below:

$$\rho_{AB} = \arccos \frac{A \cdot B}{\sqrt{\sum_{k=1}^{n} a_k^2} \sqrt{\sum_{k=1}^{n} b_k^2}} \tag{3.31}$$

where $A \cdot B$ denotes the inner product of vectors A and B.

In addition to using space node information, we can also use the network topological structure information to calculate similarity between sub-communities. As community structure is a set of nodes connected densely inside, many scholars measure the degree of similarity between the sub-community networks via neighbor nodes of information characteristic of this topology, where a typical example is the similarity based on the number of direct neighbor nodes expressed as below.

$$\omega_{ij} = \frac{|\Gamma(i) \cap \Gamma(j)|}{|\Gamma(i) \cup \Gamma(j)|} \tag{3.32}$$

$\Gamma(i)$ and $\Gamma(j)$ denote collection of a direct neighbor node of i and j respectively. $|X|$ denotes the number of elements in the set X.

The above formula depicts the degree of similarity between the community structure from different perspective and sides. Selecting the appropriate similarity formula according to different network characteristics can effectively improve the detection accuracy of the community. For example, Huang et al. [40] consider each network node as community structure which has a node and use the similarity formula (Formula 3.31) based on cosine representing the similarity between communities of the similarity between communities and detect connected closely nodes in the local area by the local notion of the strongest edges for merging. Each combined community will be deemed as a virtual node and will be involved in the subsequent merger process.

3.4.3 Label propagation algorithms

Label propagation algorithms, proposed by Zhu et al. in 2002, is a semi-supervised learning algorithm based on a graph which forecasts the information of unlabeled nodes according to information of labeled nodes [33]. Because the algorithms are simple and have low time complexity, Raghavan et al. applied them to detect communities in networks [8]. These algorithms need no specific objective functions and define community structure by intuitive heuristic rules. Some label propagation algorithms are introduced as below.

1. LPA algorithm

The basic idea of LPA algorithm is to set labels for all nodes in networks and design a propagation rule through which labels are propagated iteratively until all labels are stable. Then, nodes with the same label are partitioned into the same community. The label of each node is updated as the label with most neighbor nodes. The propagation rule defines the community structure of a network, in which each node is partitioned into the community that most neighbor nodes belong to.

Steps of the algorithm is shown as below in detail.

(1) At the beginning, initialize each node by a unique label.
(2) The label of each node is updated as the label with most neighbor nodes by scanning all nodes in a random order. If there are several labels with most neighbor nodes, select one randomly.
(3) If the label of each node is the same as the label with most neighbor nodes, go to step (4); otherwise, return to step (2).
(4) Finally, regard each connected part with the same label as a community.

Apply the LPA algorithm to the example in this chapter. The propagation process of labels is shown in Figure 3.16, which can be described as below.

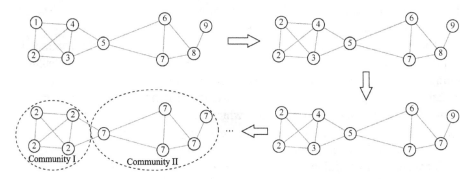

Figure 3.16: The propagation of labels on the example.

(1) In the beginning, label each node by its own node number.
(2) Generate a random order {1, 8, 6, 5, 7, 3, 2, 4, 9} for all nodes. Then scan all nodes in this order and update labels according to the updating rule.
(3) After scanning in this order, the label of each node is the same as the label with most neighbor nodes, i.e., all labels in the network are stable.
(4) According to different labels of nodes, the network can be partitioned into two communities, i.e., {1, 2, 3, 4} and {5, 6, 7, 8, 9}.

In this algorithm, to avoid the algorithm cycle and ensure convergence, reorder nodes randomly and update labels asynchronously before each propagation. The community structure may be nonunique according to this rule. Several community structures may satisfy the stop condition according to the same initial condition. But they are similar to each other. Figure 3.17 shows two possible community structures of the example. Node 5 has two neighbors in both two communities. As a result, it can be partitioned into either community I or community II. A community structure with more information can be generated by merging labels of a node in different community structures into one.

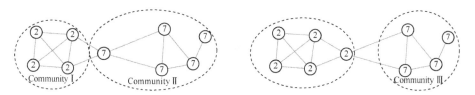

Figure 3.17: Two possible community structures of the example.

The algorithm can detect communities naturally according to the topological structure of networks without any parameters including the number and the size of communities. Besides, the time complexity is almost linear. The time complexity for initializing each node is $O(n)$. In each iteration, for each node x, group its neighbors by their labels; then update the label of node according to the label of its largest neighbor group. This process costs $O(d_x)$, where d_x denotes the degree of node x. Repeat this process for each node and the time complexity in each iteration is $O(n\bar{d})$, i.e., $O(m)$. Experiments show that the number of iteration need for the convergence of algorithm is usually independent from the size of a network. In general, 95% nodes will be partitioned correctly after 5 iterations. Therefore, the time complexity of this algorithm is very low which is approximately $O(n)$ on sparse networks. The core idea of this algorithm is similar to the formation of communities in online social network to some extent. In online social networks, users tend to participate in the same subject as its most neighbors, which forms communities in networks. Appearance of communities only depends on the local information of networks. As a result, LPA algorithm is suitable for community detection in large online social networks.

2. An extension of LPA algorithm for overlapping communities

In the original LPA algorithm, a node has only one label in the process of label propagation. Hence, a node belongs to only one community finally and the community structure discovered by the algorithm is nonoverlapping. To fit for the overlapping community structure in online social networks, Steve Gregory extended LPA algorithm and proposed the COPRA algorithm [34].

The algorithm improved the process of label propagation, and allows for multiple labels for each node to contain the information of multiple communities. To give each node accurately with multiple labels, Steve Gregory provided a belongingness coefficient b of each label c for each node, which composes a relationship pair (c, b). Belongingness coefficient b also denotes the intensity of belongingness of a node to community c. As a result, all coefficients need to be normalized. During label propagation, labels of each node are updated as the union sets of its neighbor labels, then normalize the belongingness coefficients of each node. As shown in Figure 3.18, some of the nodes {3, 4, 5, 6, 7} in the network are selected to operate the label propagation. In the beginning, each node has only one label with belongingness coefficient 1. Labels of each node will be updated as the union sets of its neighbor labels and the belongingness coefficients of each node will be normalized after an iteration. In this case, each node can keep all the labels. To remove these unimportant labels, a threshold value v can be set to delete the labels with belongingness coefficient smaller than $1/v$ to ensure each node has v labels at most, i.e., it can belong to v communities at most. As a result, v also denotes the largest number of communities that a node belongs to.

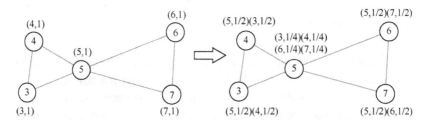

Figure 3.18: A propagation iteration of labels in the network composed of {3, 4, 5, 6, 7}.

Time complexity of the algorithm in each iteration on sparse networks is $O(v^3 n + vn\log(v))$. For an online social network, v denotes the largest number of communities that a node belongs to, which is a constant much smaller than the size of networks n. Therefore, the time complexity of the algorithm in each iteration is almost linear.

3. Improving the stability of LPA algorithm

Although LPA algorithm is simple and has low time complexity, it is an uncertainty algorithm. Leung et al. found that, after using asynchronous updated LPA algorithm for many times, a variety of community structure may be obtained for the same online social network. In some structures, there is a community with particularly large scale. The community may contain more than 50% of the nodes in a network [35]. Because when the edge density in some communities is not high enough, its internal label may have been invaded by other communities, which generates a huge community.

To solve this problem, Leung et al. proposed an algorithm to improve the LPA algorithm [35]. The original updating rule of LPA does not consider the propagation distance. No matter how far the label propagates, the effect on the updating of other labels is invariable. As a result, the label in a community can propagate very far to invade other communities and generate a large community. In the improved algorithm, Leung et al. assigned a score for each label which decreases with the increase of label propagation distance. Using the score to weight the influence of label's propagation process, the influence of scores to the update other labels will gradually become smaller along with the increase of label propagation distance, thus effectively preventing a label from propagating too far and invading other communities.

Another important reason of the instability of LPA algorithm is the randomness in the process of the algorithm. For example, when label is updated asynchronously, each iteration of algorithm needs a new random sequence. Therefore, when executing the algorithm on the same dataset for multiple times, the update order of nodes is different, which may lead to multiple different community structures. Zhao et al. designed a label propagation algorithm LPA-E based on the entropy order. The algorithm uses the label entropy in an ascending order in each iteration of label propagation and removes the randomness in original algorithm to make the community structure more stable [36].

To make the community structure more stable and reasonable, Lou et al. proposed an improved LPA algorithm based on coherent neighborhood propinquity (CNP) [37]. When updating node labels, they introduced the CNP between nodes to measure the propinquity of any node pair in networks. When updating the label, they used CNP between nodes to weight node labels. Two nodes are more close to each other and the mutual effect between their labels is greater as the CNP value between them is larger. When updating labels, the label with biggest CNP value is updated. The idea that nodes who are more close to each other have greater mutual influence in the process of label propagation also conforms to online social networks. Users who are more close to a certain user have greater influence on community selection of the user, i.e., users tend to choose the community that their intimate partners participate in.

3.4.4 Local expansion optimization algorithms

Virtual community structure is the local structure in online social networks. The formation of a virtual community only depends on connecting the relation of local network and has nothing to do with topological structure in other areas of the network. Therefore, the algorithm based on local topological information is more in line with the characteristics of the virtual community in online social networks. This algorithm defines a health function based on the local topological structure of network. It starts with a seed community and iteratively extends the seed community until the health function is optimized which forms an optimal natural community. Natural communities extended by different seed communities overlap with each other. Therefore, this algorithm can detect the overlapping community structure of networks and is suitable for detecting overlapping communities in online social networks. Several local expansion optimization algorithms are described as below.

1. LFM algorithm

Lancichinetti et al. proposed LFM algorithm according to the optimization of the local expansion. The algorithm starts from a seed community and iteratively discovers natural communities of all nodes which forms the final partition of communities in networks. Natural community of nodes is defined as the subgraph which has the largest health degree. Therefore, adding a new node in the subgraph or deleting a node from the subgraph will decrease the health degree of the subgraph. The health degree of subgraph G is defined below.

$$f_G = \frac{\kappa_{in}^G}{\left(\kappa_{in}^G + \kappa_{out}^G\right)^\alpha} \tag{3.33}$$

In this formula, κ_{in}^G and κ_{out}^G, respectively, denote the sum of internal and external degree of all nodes in subgraph G. α is a positive real parameter used to control the size of discovered community. According to health degree of the subgraph, the health degree of node A in a subgraph G is defined below.

$$f_G^A = f_{G+\{A\}} - f_{G-\{A\}} \tag{3.34}$$

In this formula, $f_{G+\{A\}}$ and $f_{G-\{A\}}$, respectively, denote the health degree including node A and without node A in subgraph G.

Specific steps for discovering natural community of node A are as follow.

Input: the value of parameter α.

(1) Initially, natural community G of node A only includes A;

(2) Implement a cycle to all neighbors which are not in G and calculate the health degree of each node with respect to G. If the maximal health degree is positive, add the node which has the maximum health degree into G. Otherwise, the algorithm ends and output the natural community G of A;

(3) Recalculate the health degree of all nodes in G;

(4) If the minimal health degree is negative, delete the node with minimal health degree from G and turn back to step (3). Otherwise turn back to step (2).

Steps of finding natural community of node 1 in the example in this chapter by the algorithm are as follow.

Input: parameter $\alpha = 1$.

(1) Initially, natural community G of node 1 only includes node 1;
(2) Implement a cycle to all neighbor nodes {2, 3, 4} which are not in G and calculate all neighbor nodes' health degree with respect to G. It is found that the maximal health degree is 2 and $f_G^2 = 0.33$. Thus, add node 2 into G.
(3) Recalculate the health degree of each node in G;
(4) At this time, the health degree of each node in G is positive. Then, continue to calculate the health degree of each neighbor node with respect to G.

Expansion process of natural community of node 1 is shown in Figure 3.19. T denotes the number of iterations in expansion process. When G is {1, 2, 3, 4, 5}, the maximal local health degree is $f_G = 0.89$.

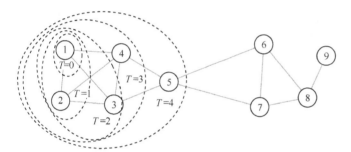

Figure 3.19: Expansion process of natural community of node 1.

The parameter α in the health degree function is very important as it can control the resolution to find communities. Large α will result in small communities, and for small α the situation is reversed. Existing experiments show that, under most circumstances, if $\alpha < 0.5$, the network can only be partitioned into a single community. However, if $\alpha > 2$, we can get minimal community structure in networks. A natural way of choosing value for α is 1, which can make the definition of health degree and weak community structures the same [38]. Under most circumstances, the corresponding community structure with $\alpha = 1$ is relatively more important for it reveals key information of real network community structures. Because different parameter resolution correspond to different community scales, this algorithm can be adopted to explore community structures in different levels.

Similar to label propagation algorithm, this algorithm is a nondeterministic one as well. Because it may find different community structures when selecting seed node with different orders. The execution time of it largely depends on the community scale and degree of overlapping between communities. To establish a natural community with scale of s, the algorithm requires a time complexity of approximately $O(s^2)$, therefore, for a fixed value a, the time complexity of the algorithm is $O(n_c \langle s^2 \rangle)$, where n_c is the number of natural communities and $\langle s^2 \rangle$ is the second-order moment. So the algorithm has approximately linear time complexity as the scale of community is relatively smaller than scale of networks. With respect to online social communities, the scale of virtual community is generally smaller than the scale of networks, resulting in a relatively small time complexity of the algorithm, so this algorithm is suitable for analysis in large scale networks.

2. GCE algorithm

LFM algorithm utilizes nodes as seeds to expand communities. It deletes nodes with negative health degree during this expanding procedure. To reduce the computational complexity, LFM only find the natural communities of nondistributed nodes, instead of finding communities of all nodes. However, in this manner, the communities of each node may be few, which leads to the low degree of overlapping in the community structures. In fact, overlapping degree of communities depends on the number of nodes that belong to different communities simultaneously. In social networks, every user can join in arbitrary amount of virtual communities based on their personal interests. Thus, there exists high overlapping degree in online social networks. However, most overlapping community detection algorithms will be effective only under the circumstance that the degree of overlapping is low. With respect to this problem, Lee et al. suggested GCE algorithm (another local expansion optimization algorithm), which is more suited for highly overlapped communities [39].

GCE algorithm finds a set of seeds at first and then expands these seeds to form a community using greedy algorithm to optimize a local health function. Finally, it accepts the communities that are not similar to the existing ones. GCE algorithm applies the same local health function as the one used by LFM algorithm. Contrary to LFM algorithm, this algorithm uses maximum cliques as seeds. In the content that follows, we will call maximum clique as clique for short. Inside the implementation procedure of the algorithm, small cliques is not desired as seeds, so a threshold value k should be used to discard unqualified cliques. After obatining all cliques, the algorithm places all neighbor nodes into cliques with the help of greedy local optimization health function until corresponding health function of subgraph reaches maximum. By expanding all groups to form communities, this algorithm can find highly overlapping community structures. However, different groups may result in same or similar communities. To deal with the same or similar communities, this algorithm discards new communities that are same as or similar to existing communities during the procedure when finding seed communities sequentially.

3.5 Summary

Recently, with the development of social network services such as Facebook, Twitter, and Sina Weibo, online social networks have gradually become the focus of research from various fields. Virtual community detection in online social network is an important part of social network analysis. Analyzing the community structure and composition in social networks helps in investigating the characteristics of the topological structure of social network, finding user's clustering patterns and influence factors, boosting information indexing, information recommendation, information propagation and control, and public security events, among others. Therefore, research concerning community detection algorithms has important social meaning and application value.

Based on the various characteristics of online social networks and the traditional complex network community theory, this chapter summarized the definition of community structure and categorized the mainstream community detection algorithms into static and dynamic calculation detection algorithms. Finally, we discussed related studies in virtual community detection algorithms.

Even if algorithms and technologies of community detection have achieved tremendous theoretical and application success, we think it still requires in-depth research in the following aspects:

1. At present, majority of community detection algorithms are proposed against static social network, i.e., the network structure does not change with time. However, online social network is a continuously changing dynamic network. New nodes and edges are added continuously. Thus, a more challenging task is to find community structure in dynamic social networks. An intuitive approach in dynamic social networks is to enforce snapshot, which is mapped to certain static topological structure at a certain time point. This approach can find community structures in social networks at different times and detect the evolution law of structure in networks. However, it has bad resistance against noise in networks, and the algorithm should have high time complexity for it to be operated on each snap. Consequently, it is not suitable for community detection in online social networks in time. Therefore, it is necessary to develop efficient virtual community detection approaches and technologies in dynamic social networks based on "increment" data in networks.

2. Most virtual community detection algorithms available currently are based on modifications of traditional algorithms in complex networks, which is only applicable to homogeneous network structures, i.e., networks with only a single type of nodes and edges. As products of the combination of real social networks and internet technology, edges and nodes of online social networks may have multiple types. For example, nodes can denote users, information (photos, labels, etc.), and edges can also denote the relationships between users, the relationships between users and labels, the relationships between photos and labels, etc. Different kinds

of nodes and edges provide us with rich and valuable information. However, it also presents an obstacle in how to deal with them properly. Therefore, the diversity of nodes and edges brings us new challenges as well as opportunities in developing excellent virtual community detection algorithms.

References

[1]   Newman M: Fast algorithm for detecting community structure in networks. Phys Rev E 2004, 69:066133.
[2]   Kernighan BW, Lin S: An efficient heuristic procedure forpartitioning graphs. Bell Syst Tech J 1970, 49:291–307.
[3]   Fiedler M: A property of eigenvectors of nonnegative symmetricmatrices and its application to graph theory. Czech Math J 1977, 25:619–633.
[4]   Newman M, Girvan M: Finding and evaluating community structure in networks. Phys Rev E 2004,69:026113.
[5]   Rosvall M, Bergstrom C: Maps of random walks on complex networks reveal community structure. Proc Natl Acad Sci 2008, 105:1118–1123.
[6]   Palla G, Derényi I, Farkas I, Vicsek T: Uncovering the overlapping community structure of complex networks in nature and society. Nature 2005, 435:814–818.
[7]   Lancichinetti A, Fortunato S, Kertész J: Detecting the overlapping and hierarchical community structure of complex networks. New J Phys 2009, 11:033015.
[8]   Raghavan NU, Albert R, Kumara S: Near linear time algorithm to detect community structures in large-scale networks. Phys Rev E 2007, 76:036106.
[9]   Fortunato S: Community detection in graphs. Phys Rep 2010, 486.
[10]   Danon LV, Duch J, Arenas A, Diaz-Guilera A: Comparing community structure identification. <i>J Stat Mech Theory Exp</i> 2005, 09008.
[11]   Rand W: Objective criteria for the evaluation of clustering method. J Am Assoc 1971, 66:846–850.
[12]   Zachary W: An information flow model for conflict and fission insmall group. J Anthropol Res 1977, 33:452–473.
[13]   Lancichinetti A, Fortunato S: Benchmarks for testing community detection algorithms on directed and weighted graphs with overlapping communities. Phys Rev E 2009, 80:016118.
[14]   Shen H, Cheng X, Cai K, Hu M: Detect overlapping and hierarchical community structure. Physica A 2008, 388:1706–1712.
[15]   Guimera R, Sales-Pardo M, Amaral LN: Modularity from fluctuations in random graphs and complex networks. Phys Rev E 2004,70:025101.
[16]   Duch J, Arenas A: Community detection in complex networks using extremal optimization. <i>Phys Rev E</i> 2005;72:027104.
[17]   Blondel VD, Guillaume JL, Lambiotte R, Lefebvre E: Fast unfolding of communities in large networks. J Stat Mech 2008, 2008:P10008.
[18]   Zhao Y, Jiang W, Li S, Ma Y, Su G, Lin X: Nerocomputing 2013.
[19]   Du J, Lai J, Shi C: Multi-objective optimization for overlapping community selection. Advanced Data Mining and Applications, 2013.
[20]   Shi C, Yu P, Yan Z, Huang Y, Wang B: Comparison and selection of objective functions in multi-objective community detection. Comput Intell 2013, 30:562–582.

[21] Gong M, Ma L, Zhang Q, Jiao L: Community detection in networks by using multiobjective evolutionary algorithm with decomposition. Physica A 2012, 391:4050–4060.

[22] Newman M, Leicht E: Mixture models and exploratory analysis in networks. Proc Natl Acad Sci 2007, 104:9564–9569.

[23] Ren W, Yan G, Liao X, Xiao L: Simple probabilistic algorithm for detecting community structure. Phys Rev E 2009,79:036111.

[24] Blei D, Ng A, Jordan M: Latent Dirichlet Allocation. J Mach Learn Res 2003, 3:993–1022.

[25] Yu L, Wu B, Wang B: LBLP: Link-clustering-based approach for overlapping community detection. Tsinghua Sci Tech 2013, 18.

[26] Kim Y, Jeong H: Map equation for link communities. Phys Rev E 2011, 84:026110.

[27] Adamic L, Glance N: The Political Blogosphere and the 2004 U.S. Election: Divided They Blog. In Proceedings of the WWW-2005 Workshop on the Weblogging Ecosystem, 2005.

[28] Rosvall M, Axelsson D, Bergstrom C: The map equation. Eur Phys J 2009, 178.

[29] Jin S, Li A, Yang S, Lin W, Deng B, Li S. A MapReduce and Information Compression based Social Community StructureMining Method. In 16th International Conference on Computational Science and Engineering, 2013.

[30] Farkas I, Ábel D, Palla G, Vicsek T: Weighted network modules. New J Phys 2007, 9:180.

[31] Onnela JP, Saramäki J, Kertész J, Kaski K: Intensity and coherence of motifs in weighted complex networks. Phys Rev E 2005, 71:065103.

[32] Kumpula J, Kivelä M, Kaski K, Saramäki J: Sequential algorithm for fast clique percolation. Phys Rev E 2008, 78:026109.

[33] Zhu X, Ghahramani Z: Learning from labeled and unlabeled data with label propagation. Technical report, CMU CALD tech report CMU-CALD-02, 2002.

[34] Gregory S: Finding overlapping communities in networks by label propagation. New J Phys 2012, 12:103018.

[35] Leung I, Hui P, Liò P, Crowcroft J: Towards real-time community detection in large networks. Phys Rev E 2009, 79:066107.

[36] Zhao Y, Li S, Chen X: Community detection using label propagation in entropic order. 12th International Conference on Computer and Information Technology, 2012.

[37] Lou H, Li S, Zhao Y: Detecting community structure using label propagation with weighted coherent neighborhood propinquity. Physica A 2013, 392:3095–3105.

[38] Radicchi F, Castellano C, Cecconi F, Loreto V, Parisi D: Defining and identifying communities in networks. Proc Natl Acad Sci 2004, 101:2658–2663.

[39] Lee C, Reid F, McDaid A, Hurley N: Detecting highly overlapping community structure by greedy clique expansion. In Proc. SNAKDD Workshop, 2010: 33–42.

[40] Huang J, Sun H, Han J, Feng B: Density-based shrinkage for revealing hierarchical and overlapping community structure in networks. Physica A 2011, 390:2167–2171.

[41] Traud A, Kelsic E, Mucha P, Porter M: Comparing community structure to characteristics in online collegiate social networks. SIAM Rev 2011, 53:526–543.

Xueqi Cheng
4 Evolution analysis of virtual communities

4.1 Introduction

In social network researches, research on the structure of virtual communities has attracted wide attention from scientists. Virtual communities that form a social network are groups or clusters, reflecting the characteristic of gathering locally form individual behaviors in the network. There are numerous explicit or implicit virtual community structures in online social networks, such as circles in renren.com and groups in douban. com. The structures of these virtual communities are not immutable but evolve over time with online social network structure. Traditional researches on the structure of virtual communities focus on static network. With big data, access and analysis of large-scale evolution data in dynamic network has become possible, and it has become a trend to turn from analyzing static networks to researching the evolution of dynamic networks in recent social network researches. The evolution of virtual communities is closely related with the functions of social networks such as diffusion, invulnerability, cooperation, and synchronization, playing a fundamental role in the evolution of the social network. Therefore, the issues regarding the evolution of virtual communities in the social network are important. This chapter mainly introduces content related to the evolution of virtual communities. This chapter is organized as follows: Section 4.2 introduces three basic mechanisms for the merging of virtual communities, i.e., period closure, preference connection, and aging factors; Section 4.3 further analyzes the effects of structural diversity of individuals from the aspect of accumulative effect by individuals joining virtual communities, and then considers the effects of structural balancing factors on the evolutions of virtual communities. Finally, Section 4.4 introduces the detection algorithm for evolving virtual community based on the similarity comparison at adjacent moments, evolution clustering analysis, Laplacian dynamics, clique percolation algorithm, trend analysis on node behaviors, along with other typical dynamic virtual community detection algorithms.

4.2 Merging of virtual communities

An important structural characteristic during the merging of virtual communities is clustering phenomenon in network, which exists in many real networks such as social network, World Wide Web, reference network, and scientist cooperation network. This section mainly introduces the effects of period closure, preference connection, aging factors along with other mechanisms in the merging of virtual communities on the clustering phenomenon, and also introduces some related models.

https://doi.org/10.1515/9783110599374-004

4.2.1 Period closure in merging of virtual communities

An important topological structural characteristic of social network is that every edge has different weights with different physical meanings, such as closeness of relationship and frequency of interaction. In addition social network, many networks can be depicted by weighted network, such as transportation network, metabolism network, and other connectivity-based networks. In such networks, the weight of edge has an important effect on the nature and function of network, such as disease transmission [1], synchronization dynamics of vibrator [2], and statistics of die body [3]; whereas the weight of edge has an important effect on the merging of virtual community in social network.

In social network, we call connections between close friends as strong and connections between friends that have distant relationship or meet once in a while as weak. Strong and weak connections are two important types of edge [4]. As shown in previous studies, the topological structure of large-scale social network satisfies weak connection assumption [4], i.e., strong connections mostly appears inside virtual community in network and weak connections mostly appears between virtual communities. As shown by studies, topological structure such as online social network is formed through the microevolution of two kinds of social networks, i.e., period closure and focus closure [5].

Period closure refers to the structure formed as nodes in network establish connection with the neighbor of its neighbor in the network, which is the main factor in the formation of a virtual community. As shown in an experiment, the probability of ternary closure decreases exponentially with the increase in geodesic distance between two nodes. In contrast, focus closure is independent of geodesic distance, but is generated by the common interests or activities of two nodes.

By combining the above two microevolution mechanisms of social network, Kumpula et al. proposed the merging model of weighted virtual community [6] with the algorithm mainly comprising three steps (Algorithm 4.1), as shown in Figure 4.1.

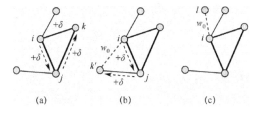

(a)   (b)   (c)

Figure 4.1: Merging algorithm of weighted virtual community [(a) and (b) show local connection mechanism and (c) shows the overall connection mechanism (see Reference [6])].

(1) Local connection mechanism: During time interval Δt, each node i connects with one of its neighbor node j at the probability of $w_{i,j}/s_i$, where $w_{i,j}$ denotes the weight of i, j connection and $s_i = \sum j w_{i,j}$ denotes the weight of node i. If the selected node j

has other neighbor nodes besides i, randomly select a node k from them at probability $w_{j,k}/(s_j - w_{i,j})$. If there is no other edge between nodes i and k, generate the edge between i and k at the probability of $p_\Delta \Delta t$ with the weight of $w_{i,k} = w_0$; otherwise, the weight of this edge increase by δ. $w_{i,j}$ and $w_{j,k}$ increases by δ regardless of whether edge exists between i and k. The above process reflects the period closure mechanism.

(2) Overall connection mechanism: If a node has neighbor nodes, such a node connects to a randomly-selected node at a probability of $p_r \Delta t$ to form an edge with weight of w_0; otherwise, such a node connects to a randomly-chosen node to form an edge with weight of w_0. This process is similar to focus closure as a node other than the neighbor node of the selected node is selected.

(3) Removal mechanism: Remove all nodes and its connected edges at the probability of $p_d \Delta t$ and replace the removed node with a new node to maintain the total number of nodes constant.

where the proportion of p_Δ and pr reflect the internal density of the network community generated from this model. The weight of network edge can be adjusted by parameter δ. When $\delta=0$, an unweighted network is generated from this model. When $\delta > 0$ increases monotonically, the internal density of the network community generated from this model increases and the internal edge weight of community increases due to the local edge mechanism. With the increase in δ, after some edges are selected, the edge weight of its triangles increases rapidly, allowing the edges of these triangles to be easily selected repeatedly, thereby forming a community

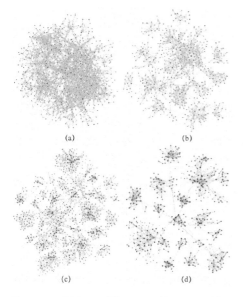

(a)

(b)

(c)

(d)

Figure 4.2: (a) $\delta = 0$, (b) $\delta = 0.1$, (c) $\delta = 0.5$, (d) $\delta=1$ network structural graph [edge color from light color (weak connection) to dark color (strong connection) (see Reference [6])].

structure with dense connections around those triangles. Figure 4.2 shows the structural graph of network generated using this model through different parameters.

Network generated from this model not only has a community structure with adjustable density but also has some typical characteristics of a real social network:
(1) Degree distribution follows exponential distribution with asymmetry.
(2) Nodes with big degree in network tend to connect other nodes with big degree and represent positive correlation.
(3) The network has high clustering coefficient of $c(k)\sim 1/k$.
(4) The network has an average diameter of $\log N$ and represent small-world phenomenon.

4.2.2 Preference connection in merging of virtual communities

Social network, like many other complex networks (e.g., metabolism network, computer network), represents small-world phenomenon and follows power-law distribution. Duncan Watts and Steven Strogatz first proposed the WS small-world model for modeling network with high aggregation; Albert-László Barabási and Réka Albert first proposed the BA model for modeling network with power-law distribution. However, neither WS nor BA model can model social network with both high aggregation and power-law distribution. This section mainly introduces two types of model for modeling social network with both high aggregation and power-law distribution.

Type I is clustering scale-free network model [7] proposed by Holme et al. First, we define network $G = (V,E)$, where V denotes the set of all nodes in network and E denotes the set of all edges in network. We assume that there is no multi-edge between any two nodes and clustering coefficient of the network is $y=\langle y_v \rangle$, where $\langle \cdot \rangle$ denotes the average of all node clustering coefficients. The clustering coefficient y_v of node v is defined as follows: assume the degree of node v is k_v, then the possible number of edges among k_v nodes is $k_v(k_v-1)/2$; define $|\xi(\Gamma_v)|$ as the number of actual edges among those nodes, then $y_v = 2|\xi(\Gamma_v)|/k_v(k_v-1)$. If $y=1$, the network is fully connected and the clustering coefficient of network generated from BA model is $y \approx 0$, thus, it has no small-world phenomenon.

The algorithm of clustering scale-free model is as follows (Algorithm 4.2): To generate power-law distribution, first introduce the following BA model mechanism into clustering scale-free model.
(a) The initial network has m_0 nodes but no edge.
(b) Add 1 node v in network in each step which connects to m edges.
(c) The probability for connecting each new node v to an existing node w is $P_w = k_w/\sum_v \in Vk_v$.

(d) To generate high aggregation characteristic, the following preference connection mechanism is added to this model.

If node v connects to w in the above step (c), randomly selects a neighbor node of w for connecting to v. If all neighbor nodes of w are connected to v already, return to step (c).

In each loop, the algorithm first carry out step (b) and (c), then carry out step (d) at the probability of P_t and step (c) at the probability of $1-P_t$. The average number of triangles connected to each node is $m_t = (m-1)P_t$, where m_t denotes control parameter of this model. When $m_t = 0$, the clustering scale-free network model degenerates into BA model, as shown in Figure 4.3.

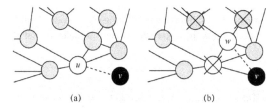

(a)   (b)

Figure 4.3: (a) In step (c) of clustering scale-free network model, new node v randomly connects to existing node u in network. (b) In step (d), new node v randomly connects to neighbor node w of node u. × means nodes that cannot connect to v (see Reference [7]).

First calculate the degree distribution of network generated from a clustering scale-free model. The degree increment of any node v by carrying out step (c) can be represented as:

$$\Delta k_v/\Delta t = Ak_v/\sum\nolimits_{w \in V} k_w$$

where A denotes normalization factor and k_v denotes the degree of node v. The degree increment of any node v by carrying out step (d) can be represented as:

$$\Delta k_v/\Delta t = \sum\nolimits_{w \in \Gamma_v} k_w(1/k_w)/\sum\nolimits_{w \in V} k_w = k_v/\sum\nolimits_{w \in V} k_w$$

where Γv denotes the set of neighbor nodes of node v. As mt step (d) and $m-mt$ step (c) were carried out in each loop of the algorithm of this model,

$$\Delta k_v/\Delta t = m_t(k_v/\sum\nolimits_{w \in V} k_w) + (m - m_t)(k_v/\sum\nolimits_{w \in V} k_w) = k_v/2t$$

and further

$$k_v \propto t^{\frac{1}{2}}$$

This result is the same as that of the BA model. It is easy to obtain degree distribution of the network $P(k) \sim k-3$, as shown in Figure 4.4, indicating that clustering scale-free network model can generate a network with power-law distribution but not a scale-free network with a given exponent.

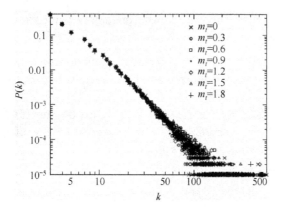

Figure 4.4: Node degree distribution of network generated from clustering scale-free network model. When the number of nodes $N=105$, $m=m_0=3$. When $m_t=0$, the degree distribution is similar to that of the BA model (see Reference [7]).

In addition, the value of parameter m_t in this model affects the proportion of triangles in the network as well as the clustering coefficient in network. Figure 4.5 (a) shows the function graph of clustering coefficient y and the number of nodes y according to different parameter m_t. We found that, for nonzero m_t, the increase of y along with N tends to nonzero finite constant. When $m_t=0$, the increase of y along with N tends to zero. Figure 4.5 (b) shows that clustering coefficient y increase monotonically along with m_t in approximate linear relation, indicating that this model can generate a network with high aggregation with clustering coefficient controlled by parameters. In addition, $l \sim \log N$ for any $m_t > 0$ indicates that this model can also generate small-world characteristic.

The next is the second type of model for modeling high aggregation and power-law distribution, i.e., acquaintance network [8] proposed by Davidsen et al. The algorithm of this model is defined as follows (Algorithm 4.3).

(a) Randomly select two neighbor nodes of a reference node and connect the two nodes if they are not connected. If the number of neighbor nodes of the selected node is less than two, randomly select another node for connecting the reference node.

(b) Randomly delete a node and all edges connected to it at a probability of p, and then randomly connect it to a node in network.

Repeat the above two steps circularly. Different from clustering scale-free network model, the number of nodes in acquaintance network model remains unchanged. The existing time of nodes in network is limited due to deletion mechanism (b), thus the whole network can finally reach an equilibrium state. The probability p determines the proportion of step (a) and step (b). In general, one person associates with other persons for several minutes or hours each time, but their relationship exists in the social network for many years. Therefore, we only consider situations when $p \ll 1$ in the following discussion.

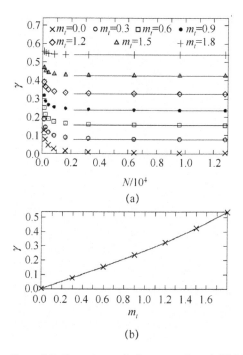

Figure 4.5: Clustering scale-free network model [(a) is the relation graph of clustering coefficient and number of nodes, (b) is the relation graph of clustering coefficient and the average number of triangles connected to each node (see Reference [7])].

Figure 4.6 shows the degree distribution of network at an equilibrium state according to different p. As the existing time of each node is finite, node degree has upper limit, thus $p(k)$ only has nonzero value in finite range. As step (a) generates triangle connection and step (b) is a Poisson process, when $p \ll 1$, $p(k)$ is determined mainly by step (a) and satisfies power-law distribution; in addition, the range of length for $p(k)$ has nonzero value increases with the decrease of p. For a relatively big p, step (b) has bigger effect on degree distribution $p(k)$, thereby generating similar exponent distribution. When $p \approx 1$, step (b) plays a main role and turns the connecting process into a Poisson process. Therefore, the acquaintance network model can model social network with power-law distribution and exponential distribution.

For clustering coefficient of model generation network, Table 4.1 gives an average degree $<k>$ for different p, secondary moment of degree $<k^2>$, average clustering coefficient C, upper limit C' of coefficient of network with the same degree distribution and without triangle connection, clustering coefficient Cr and of random graph with the same number of nodes. For any random network with the same number of nodes and average degree $<k>$, if the connecting probability of any two node is $p_{link} = <k>/(N-1)$, clustering coefficient is Cr and $=p_{link}$. Therefore, for networks with unchanged number of nodes, Cr and is directly proportional to the average degree of

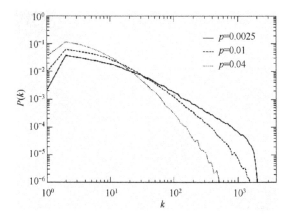

Figure 4.6: Degree distribution of network generated from acquaintance network (see Reference [8]).

network <k> (Table 4.1). For networks with the same degree distribution and random edges, Newman et al. used the function generation method of random graph and obtained the upper limit [9] of average degree coefficient of such a random network.

Table 4.1: Acquaintance network model [8].

P	$\langle k \rangle$	$\langle k2 \rangle$	C	C	Cr and
0.04	14.9	912	0.45	0.036	0.0021
0.01	49.1	13,744	0.52	0.29	0.0070
0.0025	149.2	99,436	0.63	0.43	0.021

$$C' = ((<k^2>/<k>)-1)^2/<k>N$$

For networks following Poisson degree distribution, $C' = C_{rand}$. As shown in Table 4.1, the clustering coefficient of network generated from the acquaintance network model is significantly bigger than that of the random graph with the same degree distribution.

Furthermore, the average path length of model generation network is (p=0.04) l (N) ~ logN, i.e., small-world characteristic. Newman et al. used a method to generate function and gave the approximate expression [9] of average path length l of random graph with any degree distribution as:

$$l' \approx \log(N/<k>)/\log((<k>^2-<k>)/<k>)+1$$

For networks following Poisson degree distribution

$$l_{rand} \approx logN//log<k>$$

As shown in Table 4.1, for $p = 0.0025$, $l' \approx 1.59$, lr and ≈ 1.77, $l' < lr$ and is the hub node with high degree due to a scale-free network. The value results show the average path length of network generated from acquaintance network model is $l = 2.38$, which is another strong evidence for the small-world phenomenon of such network.

4.2.3 Aging factors in merging of virtual communities

This section introduces the generation model of document network clustering phenomenon. Document network mainly includes reference network, online social network, etc., with one node denoting an article or a page containing multimedia information. The nature of document network is affected not only by its topological structure but also by the semantic relation between node content. Research on document network is important for page search and information retrieval [10–12]. This section focuses on the evolution process of document network, and investigates the effects of node similarity, node degree, aging characteristic of nodes, along with other factors on aggregation to obtain the model of clustering phenomenon of document network.

The most important model for document network research is the degree similarity mixture model [11] proposed by Filippo Menczer. Filippo Menczer first researched the correlation between document network evolution and content similarity between documents. To study the similarity between two documents, Filippo Menczer proposed the measurement formula for document content similarity:

$$\sigma_c(d_1, d_2) = \|\bar{d}_1 \cdot \bar{d}_2\| / \|\bar{d}_1\| \cdot \|\bar{d}_2\|$$

where $\bar{d}$ is the vector representation of content of d document. By researching the similarity distribution of webpage (DMOZ) and scientific article (PNAS), Menczer found that the similarity distribution of content of connected documents is significantly different from that of all documents, and that the connection probability between documents increases with the similarity of document content. Therefore, he proposed the degree similarity mixture model (DSM model) with the algorithm of model (Algorithm 4.4) as follows.

Add a new node in network each time, and the new node has $m=L/N$ edges and network node connection. At step t, the probability for connecting the new node to node i is:

$$P_r(i) = \alpha k_i / m_t + (1 - \alpha) P_r' \tag{i}$$

where $P_r'(i) \propto (1/\sigma_c(i, t) - 1)^{-\gamma}$, $i < t$, ki denotes the degree of node i, and parameter is obtained by calculating real data. The first nominal on the right side of the above formula indicates that the node tends to connect with a node with big degree in network, which is similar to the preference connection mechanism in BA model. The second nominal on the right side of the above formula indicates that the node tends to connect a node with similar content, with $0 \leq \alpha \leq 1$ as the parameter of preference connection mechanism, which controls the probability for connecting node with a big degree and similar content. If $P_r(i) = 1/t$, the new node connects to node in network in a completely random manner, which is called as the degree uniformity mixture model (DUM model). Compared with the degree uniformity mixture model, degree similarity mixture model can better fit the similarity of content of nodes in a network.

Cheng et al. discovered the triangle clustering characteristic of document network, and proposed the concept of triangle similarity and degree similarity preference model (DSP model) [13]. They first defined the connection probability $P(\sigma_c) = M^*(\sigma_c)/M(\sigma_c)$ between two documents with content similarity of σ_c, where $M(\sigma_c)$ denotes the number of node pairs with content similarity of σ_c and $M^*(\sigma_c)$ denotes the number of actually connected node pairs in network. As shown by the value results, the connection probability between two documents increases with the similarity of their content. Take PNAS reference network for example, if the similarity between two articles is $\sigma_c = 0.5$, the probability for reference relation between them is $P(\sigma_c) = 50\%$; when $\sigma_c < 0.2$, $P(\sigma_c)$ is very small. They further discovered that two documents similar to the same document are also similar, and proposed triangle similarity for describing such triangle relation of similarity, i.e., $R^{\triangle}_{ijk} = \min\{\sigma_c(i,j), \ \sigma_c(i,k), \ \sigma_c(j,k)\}$ and triangle connection probability $P(R^{\triangle})$, where $P(R^{\triangle})$ denotes the probability that three nodes with triangle similarity of $R^{\triangle}$ form a triangle. The triangle given here is a weak triangle, in which any two nodes among the three nodes have at least one directed edge. As shown in value results, triangle connection probability is sensitive to triangle similarity. For WT10g data, when the triangle similarity increases from 0.1 to 0.5, the triangle connecting probability increases by two magnitudes; for PNAS reference network data, the triangle connecting probability increases by 4 magnitudes. Cheng et al. further proposed the DSP model for document network with the algorithm (Algorithm 4.5) as follows.

(a) Expansion process of network: Add a new node in network each time at probability p determined by the number of nodes and edges in network, i.e., $p = N/(N+L)$. The average degree of nodes in network is $<k> = 2L/N = 2(1-p)/p$.

(b) DSP preference connection process: Two disconnected nodes in network connect at the probability of $1-p$. If this directed edge starts from node i and ends at j, the connection probability between i and j is:

$$\prod(i) = (k_i^{\text{out}} + \beta_1)/\sum m(k_m^{\text{out}} + \beta_1)$$

$$\prod(j) = (k_j^{\text{in}} + \beta_2)(\sigma_c(i,j) + \alpha)/\sum l[(k_l^{\text{in}} + \beta_2)(\sigma_c(i,l) + \alpha)]$$

where k_i out denotes the out-degree of node i and k_j in denotes the in-degree of node j with $i{\neq}l$, parameters β_1, β_2, α having positive value. Parameters β_1, β_2 can ensure that, at the initial stage of the algorithm, nodes with $kin=kout=0$ can connect to other nodes, whereas parameter α can ensure the connection between documents with significantly different content. All these conditions ensure that this model conforms to the actual situations.

Compared to DSM model, DSP model can better fit the structural characteristic of document network, such as degree distribution and average clustering coefficient. In addition, DSP model has advantages regarding the fitting the function relation of triangle connection probability and triangle similarity.

Ren et al. considered that the merging of clustering phenomenon in document network is affected by not only document similarity, document popularity (or the number of document edges) but also aging factors of nodes. Based on this, they proposed degree and age preference connection – clique neighbor preference connection model (DAC model) [14]. The algorithm of this model (Algorithm 4.6) is mainly comprises two parts.

(a) Degree and age preference connection: The connection probability of a new node i and an existing node j is $\Pi_{ij} {\propto} kj\ in{\times}tj{-}\alpha$, where k_j in denotes the in-degree of node j, $t_j{=}i{-}j$ denotes the age of node j, $\alpha{>}0$ denotes attenuation parameter. This probability in the form of power-law is adopted by many models, such as Dorogovtsev–Mendes (DM) model [26].

(b) Clique neighbor preference connection: All nodes of clique that nodes i and j belong to are connected at the probability of $\beta(0{\leq}\beta{\leq}1)$. If node j belongs to many cliques at the same time, randomly selects a clique s at the probability of P_s for connecting node i to all nodes in clique s, where P_s is directly proportional to the number of node in clique s. If all neighbor nodes of i can connect to i without those nodes in clique, node i can select node connection by degree and age preference connection (a) at the probability of 1-β. Obviously, β controls the increase speed of clustering coefficient in network in a directly proportional manner.

As shown in experiment results, DAC model can well simulate in-degree distribution of reference network, scale distribution of connected components, increasing law of the number of triangles with the number of nodes in network, and function relation between average clustering coefficient and node degree. In addition, DAC model can well simulate the relation between edge density and node out-degree in network. The main advantage of this model lies in revealing the relation between time sequence characteristic (aging factors) of node and clustering phenomenon of document network.

4.3 Evolution of virtual communities

The evolution process of virtual communities in online social network is extremely complicated and faces many influencing factors. An important and challenging topic in research on social network is to mine key factor in the evolution of virtual communities. This section mainly uses empirical analysis and mathematical model to introduce the effects of three basic factors of individual user on the evolution of virtual communities, i.e., accumulative effect, structural diversity, and structural balance.

4.3.1 Accumulative effect in evolution of virtual communities

A core problem in social science research is how virtual communities evolve over time and why the scale of virtual communities increases. In the field of digitalized information, MySpace, LiveJournal, and other online social networks gradually become the mainstream platform for information network exchange along with the scale's increment of virtual communities, whereas acquisition and analysis of large-scale data generated from the evolution process of virtual communities become a difficult problem. To understand the increase of virtual communities, we will mainly carry out research on the following key problems: Which factor determines a user to join a virtual community? This section introduces research results on these problems by Backstrom et al. [15]

Two datasets were adopted by Backstrom et al.: friend relationship and virtual community data on LiveJournal as well as cooperators and conference article data on DBLP. To discuss the influencing factor for a user to join a virtual community, they defined a user that has friends but had not joined the virtual community as fringe. For a fringe, Backstrom et al. first considered the relation between its probability of joining the virtual community and its number of friends in the virtual community, i.e., whether the possibility for a fringe to join the virtual community has an accumulative effect. In LiveJournal, the function relations for the probability for a fringe to join the virtual community $P(k)$ along with its number of friends in virtual community k are obtained in the following steps:

(1) Acquire two snapshots of the users included in different virtual communities for a month.
(2) Construct all ternary groups: (u, C, k), where C denotes virtual community and u doesn't belong to C in the first snapshot. At the time of the first snapshot, u has k friends in virtual community C.
(3) Given a k, $P(k)$ denotes the proportion that u belongs to the ternary group (u, C, k) of C in the second snapshot.

The function relation of $P(k)$ and k in DBLP network are obtained in a similar manner, except it acquires snapshots in a year and considers the proportion for a user to "join" a meeting in a year. Figure 4.7 and Figure 4.8 respectively give the function relation for the probability for a user to join the virtual community $P(k)$ and its number of friends in virtual community k in LiveJournal and DBLP network. The two functions

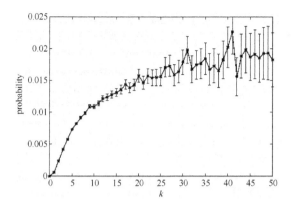

Figure 4.7: Relation graph of the probability for a user to join the LiveJournal virtual community and its number of friends in such a virtual community (see Reference [15]).

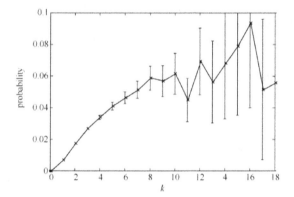

Figure 4.8: Relation graph of the probability for a user to join the DBLP virtual community and its number of friends in such a virtual community (see Reference [15]).

have similar curves and both have the "diminishing returns", i.e., monotonically increase the curve with an increasingly slower increment speed, which is completely different from "S Type" logistic function curve obtained in many propagation models. In logistic curve, $P(k)$ increases slowly with relatively small k; when k is around certain median, $P(k)$ increases faster; when k is relatively large, $P(k)$ increases slowly again. The best fitting function of this curve is $P(k)=a\log k+b$ with parameters a and b.

As shown in experiment, the top layer of the decision-making tree of LiveJournal and DBLP is very stable in many experiments and the connection situations of a user with internal friends in virtual community play an important role in prediction. The next problem to be discussed is the relation between the connection density degree with internal friends in the virtual community of a fringe and its joining such community, which can be expressed as follows: For a fringe user u with the number of edges $e(S)$ to friends in virtual community S, define the connection intensity between friends as $\varphi(S)=2e(S)/|S|(|S|-1)$, which indicates the proportion that a fringe user connects to all its friends in virtual community S, where the possible number of edges between $|S|$ friend is $|S|$ $(|S|-1)$ $/2$. As shown by the results, the fringe tends to join the virtual community when $e(S)$ and $\varphi(S)$ are large. For fixed $k=3, 4, 5$, Figure 4.9 shows the function relation between the probability of user joining the virtual community and connection intensity $\varphi(S)$, where a user tends to join the virtual community when the connection intensity between friends in the virtual community is large. According to social capital argument [16], in the same virtual community, friends knowing each other is more reliable that strangers, which indicates that a user will be supported by richer local social structure when it joins the virtual community. Therefore, the social capital argument may be an important theoretical support for the conclusion in Figure 4.9. In addition, weak connection assumption indicates that users expect to make friends with strangers in the same virtual community [17] with a possible reason that users in LiveJournal consider reliability more important than information. Backstrom et al. further inspected the function relation between the expansion speed of virtual community and triangle density therein. As shown in Figure 4.10, expansion speed of virtual community is slow when density is high, which is strange. A possible explanation for this phenomenon is that high triangle density indicates that new members in virtual community ceased to increase at a certain time in the past and only internal members connected to each other thereafter.

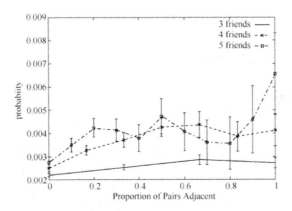

Figure 4.9: Function relation between the probability of a user joining LiveJournal virtual community and its connection degree with friends in such a community (see Reference [15]).

This section mainly discusses the evolution process of virtual community in social network overtime, including the behavior of individual joining virtual community and the overall increasing behavior of scale of virtual community. As shown in the experiment results, individual joining virtual community shows accumulative effect during the evolution process of virtual community. The next two sections will discuss more complex influencing factors in the evolution process of virtual community.

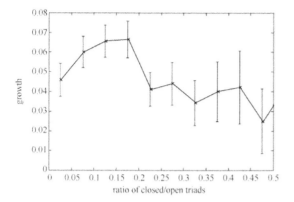

Figure 4.10: Function relation between the scale increasing speed of virtual community and ternary closure density in virtual community (see Reference [15]).

4.3.2 Structural diversity in evolution of virtual communities

Propagation process of information, virus, behavior, etc. in social network relies on the topological structure of network at different level. This section introduces research results [18] by Ugander et al. on the effect of social network structure on user behavior. Two kinds of user behaviors on Facebook is considered in this section, i.e., recruitment and engagement process; the former refers to the process that a user receives invitation email from a Facebook user and completes recruitment on Facebook; the latter refers to the process that a user engage in specific activities after such recruitment. Though both carried out on Facebook, the two processes have significant difference in specific process, and Ugander et al. mainly considered the effect of structural diversity of user nodes on the two behaviors. Structural diversity of user nodes refers to the number of user nodes of connected components which neighbor nodes in social network belong to.

Let's first analyze the recruitment process on Facebook. Assume a user A is not the user of Facebook, then users input A's email address into Facebook, so all Facebook users that A may know. Define Facebook users that has A's email address as user A's contacted neighbor users on Facebook who are subset of A's potential friends in the future (see Figure 4.11). In fact, A may know more people, but we cannot use all its friends as the sample to predict if a user will be recruited to Facebook (recruitment process) as some of them are not recruited. The recruitment process of a user on Facebook is as follows. As Facebook allows its users to send email to their friends for recruitment, which contains not only the inviter's name but also the list of all contacted users. Ugander et al. researched a basic problem by analyzing data including 54 million invitation emails: What's the relation between the probability of user recruitment on Facebook and the structure of its contacted neighbors? A traditional assumption is that the probability monotonically increase with the number of contacted neighbors, while

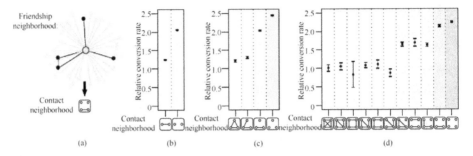

Figure 4.11: (a) Structural graph of contacted neighbors during recruitment process with nodes in light color denoting user's friends and nodes in dark color denoting user's contacted neighbors. Contacted neighbors comprise three connected components. (b~d) relative conversion ratio corresponds to two, three and four contacted neighbor graph (see Reference [18]).

the results given by Ugander et al. are that the probability of user recruitment on Facebook is only related to the connected components comprised contacted neighbors. Figure 4.12 (a) indicates the relation between Facebook user conversion ratio and the connected edge density of contacted neighbors when there is only one contacted neighbor; the results show that there is no significant relation between the two. Figure 4.12 (b) shows that the bigger the number of contacted neighbors means lower Facebook user conversion ratio under fixed number of connected components comprised contacted neighbors. In fact, the influencing factor for Facebook user conversion ratio is neither the number of inviters nor the edges between them, but the number of connected components comprised inviters, i.e., structural diversity. As connected component where each contacted neighbor locates can be deemed as different social environments, the number of different social environments in Facebook determines the probability for user recruitment on Facebook. There is an implicit social relation exists on Facebook, i.e., as figures posting photos on Facebook will be labeled, two Facebook users labeled in the same photo have social relation even though they have no connection. Figure 4.12 (c) shows that user conversion ratio is lower if two contacted neighbor nodes are labeled more times (more intense social relation) on the same photo regardless of the connection between them. Therefore, social relation intensity is the extension of social relation to a certain degree, and two users with more intense social relation have more similar social environment. More different social relation brings higher user conversion ratio, which explains the reason for lower user conversion ratio brought by higher social relation intensity between contacted neighbors. Finally, consider the effect of inviters' location in the topological structure of all contacted neighbors on user conversion ratio. Figure 4.13 shows the function relation between user conversion ratio and the topological structure of composition graph of contacted neighbors as well as inviters' location. As shown in results, the inviters' location has no significant effect of user conversion ratio, whereas acceptance probability of recruitment sent by inviters with higher node degree is slightly larger than that with lower node degree.

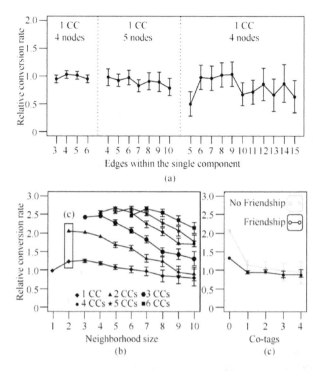

Figure 4.12: During recruitment process, (a) function relation graph between Facebook user conversion ratio and the number of edges in connected components when only one connected component comprised contacted neighbors, (b) function relation graph between user conversion ratio and the number contacted neighbors when the number of connected components comprised contacted neighbors is fixed, (c) function relation graph between user conversion ratio and the labeling times of two contacted neighbors on the same photo (see Reference [18]).

During the login process, the effects of mainly considered. Specifically, we consider whether the structural diversity in the next week after users' recruitment on Facebook in 2010 can be used to predict these users' frequent login three months after recruitment. The standard for frequent user login is Facebook login at least in 6 days out of each week. Friend scale of Facebook users is much larger than that of email. Ten million users recruited to Facebook in 2010 and the number of their friends are 10~50. In addition, as large proportion of connected components comprised users' friends are single users (nodes), it is not accurate to reflect social environment diversity by the number of connected components comprised users' friends. To reflect the diversity of social environment more accurately, we give three types of number of induced connected components. Type I number of induced connected components is the number of connected components with node number of k. Type II number of induced connected components is the number of connected components in k-core structure of neighbor nodes. Type III number of induced connected components is the number of connected components in k-brace structure of neighbor nodes. Where embeddedness of edge is

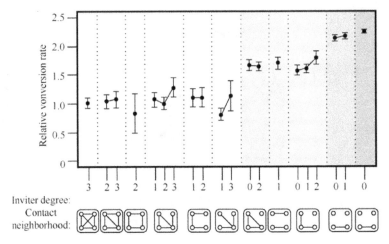

Figure 4.13: During recruitment process, function relation graph between user relative conversion ratio and topological structure of graph comprised contacted neighbors as well as location of inviter, where 4 contacted neighbors exist and the location of inviter is denoted by the node degree in graph comprised contacted neighbors. Relative conversion ratio is the ratio of actual conversion ratio or user conversion ratio when user has only one neighbor (see Reference [18]).

defined as the number of common neighbor nodes between two nodes of such edge, and the k-brace structure of a graph is defined as the sub graph after repeatedly deleting edges with embeddedness smaller than k and isolated nodes. Figure 4.14 (a) and (b) show the example of three types of parameters for measuring social environment diversity of users. Figure 4.14 (c), (d), (e) and (f) show the function relation between user Facebook login frequency and the number of induced connected components. As shown in the results, the larger the number of the above three types of induced connected components one week after user recruitment the higher user login frequency after 3 months. Therefore, the number of induced connected components can reflect the diversity of social environment that users belong to and effectively predict user login frequency. Figure 4.15 shows the relation between edge density of neighbor nodes of users and user login frequency. As shown in the results, user login frequency increases then decrease along with the increase of edge density, i.e., a peak value exists in the range of (0,1). A possible explanation for the existence of peak value is that too small edge density means lack of social environments and too large edge density means lack of diversity of social environments.

4.3.3 Structural balance in evolution of virtual communities

Social relation in social network can be classified into two types: positive relationship and negative relationship; the former refers to friendship between a user and another user or support, agreement and other positive emotional factors of a user to another user; the latter refers to the hostile relationship between a user and another user or

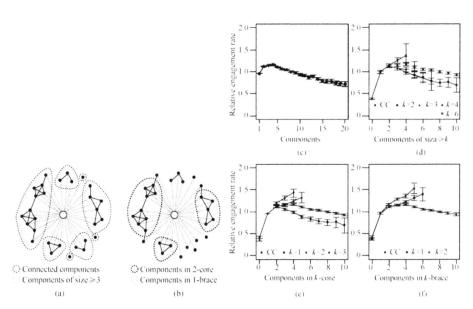

Figure 4.14: (a) Structural graph of all connected components and connected components with scale ≥3 of users' neighbors. (b) Structural graph of connected components of users' neighbors 2-core and 1-brace. (c) ~ (e) Relation graph of user relative login frequency of 50 neighbors and induced structure diversity. Relative login frequency is the ratio of actual login frequency and average user login frequency with 50 neighbors (see Reference [18]).

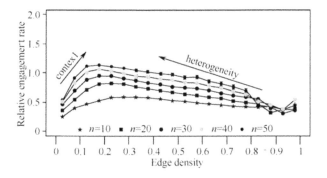

Figure 4.15: When the number of neighbors of users is respectively 10, 20, 30, 40 and 50,the function relation graph of user relative login frequency and internal connection density of neighbors (see Reference [18]).

opposition and distrust of a user to another user. Such positive and negative relationship in social network exists generally and plays an important role in environment, structure, evolution and other aspects of social network. For example, Wikipedia users can give affirmative vote or negative vote on administrator candidates; Epinions users can declare their trust or distrust on certain person; Slashdot users can declare certain person as their friends or enemies. If we denote edge of positive relationship as positive sign and edge of negative relationship as negative sign, a basic problem is that how the symbols of whole network or local network affect the symbol of an edge [19]. The meaning for researching this problem is to understand the basic principle of generating negative relationship in social network.

Gruhl et al. first proposed the symbol prediction problem [20] of single edge, i.e. how to predict the symbol of an edge with known topological structure of whole directed network and known symbols of all edges except for one edge. Formalized definition of such problem is as follows: the symbol of directed edge (x,y) from node x to node y in directed graph $G = (V,E)$, $s(x,y)$, i.e. if (x,y) has positive symbol, $s(x,y) = 1$; if (x,y) has negative symbol, $s(x,y) = -1$; if no edge exists between x and y, $s(x,y) = 0$. In some situations, we only care the symbol of directed edge and ignore its direction. If an directed edge (x,y) or (y,x) between node x and y has positive symbol while the directed edge between x and y in another direction doesn't exist or has positive symbol, then $s(x,y)=1$. In a similar way, If an directed edge (x,y) or (y,x) between node x and y has negative symbol while the directed edge between x and y in another direction doesn't exist or has negative symbol, then $\bar{s}(x,y) = -1$. The remaining situations except for the above two is denoted as $\bar{s}(x,y)=0$ (including the situation that (x,y) and (y,x) have opposite symbols). The next task is to predict $s(x,y)$ or $\bar{s}(x,y)$ with all known symbols of edges except for one directed edge (x,y). Machine learning is used in prediction method and two types of feature vector are used in prediction process. Type I feature vector has 7 features, i.e. in-edge $d_{in}+(v)$ with all symbols of node v as positive, in-edge $d_{in}-(v)$ with all symbols of node v as negative, out-edge $d_{out}+(u)$ with all symbols of node u as positive, out-edge $d_{out}-(u)$ with all symbols of node u as negative, $d_{out}+(u)+d_{out}-(u)$, $d_{in}+(v)+d_{in}-(v)$, and the number of common neighbors of u and v (or embeddedness) $C(u,v)$. Type II feature vector considers all triangles containing (u,v), which construct a 16-dimension vector as there are $2\times2\times2\times2=16$ possible different triangles for different symbols and directions. Classify the vector by Logistic regression model with probability expression as follows

$$P(+|x) = \frac{1}{1+e^{-(b_0 + \sum_i^n b_i x_i)}}$$

where $(x_1,x_2,\ldots,x_n)$ denotes feature vector and $b_0,b_1,\ldots,b_n$ denotes coefficient obtained by learning training data. As shown in experiment results, for two types of datasets, Logistic regression model can achieve good prediction by three types of feature vector (Type I feature vector, Type II feature vector, combination of Type I and Type II feature vector). As the three types of feature vector is only related to local topological structure, local topological structure characteristic is available for effective prediction of edge symbol.

Leskovec et al. further carried out symbol prediction by traditional structural balance theory [19], where some social network relations are consider to be more common and stable than other social network relations [21, 22]. Structural balance theory mainly researches the friendly or opposite relation between three persons and it is more common and stable to consider my enemy's friend as my enemy than my friend's enemy as my enemy, i.e. if triangle relationship forms between w and edge (u,v), the number of friend relationship in triangle relationship must be an odd number. In other words, a function can be defined as follows:

$$f_{balance}: \{types\tau\} \rightarrow \{+1,-1,0\}$$

where τ denotes triangle relationship (w,u,v) with $f_{balance}(\tau)=\bar{s}(u,w)\bar{s}(v,w)$. As shown in the results, the Logistic regression model combined with structural balance theory can better carry out symbol prediction on Epinions and Slashdot.

4.4 Detection of evolving virtual communities

We introduced virtual community detection algorithm in static network in Chapter 3. However, online social network changes dynamically over time, and events such as merging, disintegration, merging and splitting cause dynamic evolution of social community structure. Therefore, an important problem in virtual community research is to identify dynamically-evolving virtual community over time. In general, the task of detection of evolving virtual community is to confirm overall virtual community partition at all times or possible structural form of certain virtual community at the next moment, thereby finally identifying all evolving virtual community sequence in dynamic network by detection method for evolving virtual community. This section mainly introduces several types of basic detection algorithms for evolving virtual community in combination with general reference [23].

4.4.1 Detection of evolving virtual community based on direct similarity comparison at adjacent moments

Detection method for evolving virtual community based on direct similarity comparison at adjacent moments is the most direct method for confirming the evolving virtual community sequence in dynamic network. The underlying concept of this algorithm is as follows: First, confirm the community partition of network at adjacent moments (respectively t moment and $t+1$ moment) by virtual community detection algorithm in static network. Second, compare all detected communities in network at adjacent moments to confirm community C_t in t moment network satisfying certain similar conditions with community C_{t+1} detected at $t+1$ moment and add C_{t+1} to the evolving virtual community sequence which C_t belongs to.

Hopcroft et al. first researched the detection method for evolving virtual community [24] in dynamic reference network by the detection algorithm for evolving virtual community based on direct similarity comparison at adjacent moments. First, perform community detection on network snapshot in dynamic network sequence by hierarchical clustering algorithm with main thought as follows: Conduct merging from communities with the highest similarity until all elements are included in one community. The following including angle cosine is used to define similarity between nodes and distance between communities:

$$\text{similarity}(i, j) = \cos(r_i, r_j) = \frac{r_i \cdot r_j}{\|r_i\| \|r_j\|}$$

$$\text{dis}(C, C') = \sqrt{\frac{n_C n_{C'}}{n_C + n_{C'}}(1 - \cos(r_C, r_{C'}))}$$

where n_C denotes node scale of community C, r_i denotes property vector comprised all references of network node (article) i, and r_C denotes the normalization sum of all node property vectors in the community. To discover a stable community structure not affected by change of disturbance data, we delete a small part of nodes and edges in the tree diagram obtained in hierarchical clustering process, and define communities affected slightly as natural community. For natural communities in each network snapshot confirmed by hierarchical clustering process, we define matching degree between communities to discover the best matching natural community at adjacent moments, thereby obtaining sequence of evolving virtual community. The calculating formula of matching degree between communities is as follows:

$$\text{match}(C, C') = \min\left(\frac{|C \cap C'|}{|C|}, \frac{|C \cap C'|}{|C'|}\right)$$

The defect of above analysis method mainly appears during implementation of hierarchical clustering algorithm. As its results are unstable, few times of clustering experiment may fail to select valuable communities from hierarchical tree, thus multiple times of clustering experiments is needed. Further, this method is mainly designed for reference network, and may not be available for definitions in application of other types of dynamic networks, such as node similarity and distance between communities. Reference [25] gives a more general description of method for those defects. Based on the evolution analysis method in References [25] and [26] give a more logic definition of evolution events in various communities.

In general, this kind of method is intuitive and easy to operate but has some accuracy problems, i.e., incorrect results [27]. For example, for two communities A_t and B_t in given network with no overlapped nodes, when A_t expands to sufficient scale, A_{t+1} may have overlapped nodes with B_{t+1} (while they belong to different communities in detection algorithm of static virtual community). Such overlap between communities may make the similarity between A_{t+1} and B_t higher than that between A_{t+1} and A_t. Therefore, according to optimal similarity principle, A_{t+1} is included in the sequence of evolving virtual community where Bt belongs to, which leads to incorrect results in members of evolving virtual community.

4.4.2 Detection of evolving virtual community based on evolution clustering analysis

Detection of evolving virtual community based on direct similarity comparison at adjacent moments mainly carry out independent community detection on network snapshot at adjacent moments to obtain the evolution sequence of virtual community. However, this method can lead to significant changes in community structures at adjacent moments in the evolution sequence of virtual community. It is possible that such a significant change is not caused by the dynamic evolution of network. For this defect, based on the clustering method of static network community detection, Reference [28] proposed evolution clustering analysis frame, which can carry out detection of evolving virtual community on dynamic network sequence with the same scale. The basic principle of evolution clustering is to determine the community partition of current network according to the structure of current network and community partition of previous network. This method ensures both good partition of current network and little difference from the community partition of the previous network. References [29] and [30] rephrased spectral analysis clustering technology under the evolution clustering analysis frame. Based on evolution clustering, Lin et al. introduced an analysis frame which allowed a node to belong to multiple communities at the same time to partition dynamic community evolving over time [31]. This model can be used to discover the best community partition results to fit observation data and time sequence evolution.

This model mainly considers two kinds of factors when evaluating community partition quality, i.e. snapshot cost (SC) and temporal cost (TC). SC is defined as Kullback–Leibler divergence of similarity matrix of nodes of network at certain moment and community partition results at this moment, and bigger SC brings worse community partition. TC is defined as Kullback–Leibler divergence of community partition results of network at adjacent moment, and bigger TC brings bigger fluctuation of social partition results at adjacent moments. We optimize the following target function to discover the optimal community partition:

$$\cos t = \alpha \cdot SC + (1 - \alpha) \cdot TC$$

where α is the parameter for balancing the two factors.

In general, the analysis of evolving community based on evolution clustering technology combines the detection of optimal community partition of network with member selection of sequence of evolving community. The sequence of evolving community results obtained ensures both close connection between communities at adjacent moments in the sequence and accuracy of network partition. However, the results obtained are evolution sequence of the overall structure of network community, not specific to evolution analysis of a certain community.

4.4.3 Detection of evolving virtual community based on Laplacian dynamics

Social network usually has multiple types of nodes or edges due to its complex structure, i.e. heterogeneous network. Reference [32] first researches partition method for network communities with different types of edges. Reference [33] mainly focuses on the stability of communities affected by Laplacian dynamics factors. Based on this, Reference [34] proposed a method available for detecting multislice network community with heterogeneous structure. This method considers intracommunity connection (adjacent matrix) and interslice coupling to propose quality evaluation function similar to modularity and is available for multislice network. "Slice" in multslice network may be network structure in the same network at different moments or the slices of multiple networks in a combined network with different types of edges. In a multislice network, node sets are fixed and edges include intracommunity connection and interslice coupling. Multislice network is shown in Figure 4.16.

We define community as a node set under certain time scale in which node randomly walks but cannot walk out. For the construction of multislice network Null model, we consider the possibility of reaching node i in s slice from node j in r slice when node j reach equilibrium state, which is discussed in the following two scenarios:

1. i, j at the same slice (adjacent);
2. i, j at different slices (coupling).

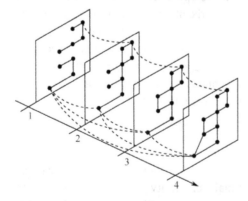

Figure 4.16: Graph of multislice network. There are 4 slices in this network with full line denoting edges between intracommunity nodes and dottedline denoting coupling of interslice nodes (see Reference [34]).

Finally, we consider the intraslice and interslice movement respectively and obtain corresponding null model:

$$\rho_{is|jr}P_{jr}{}^* = \left[\delta_{rs}\frac{k_{is}}{2m_s}\frac{k_{jr}}{k_{jr}} + \delta_{ij}\frac{C_{jrs}}{C_{jr}}\frac{C_{jr}}{k_{jr}}\right].P_{jr}^*$$

Apply equilibrium nature of Markov random walk proposed by Lambiotte et al. in 2008:

$$Q_{multislice}(t) = \sum_{i,j\in c}\left[\left(e^{t(Q-1)}\right)_{ij}P_j^* - P_i^*P_j^*\right]$$

$$= \sum_{i,j\in c}\left[\left(e^{t(Q-1)}\right)_{ij}P_{jr}^* - \rho_{is|jr}P_{jr}^*\right]$$

$$= \sum_{i,j\in c}\left[\left(\frac{A_{ijs}\delta_{rs} + C_{jrs}\delta_{ij}}{k_{jr}}\right)\frac{k_{jr}}{2u} - \gamma\left(\delta_{rs}\frac{k_{is}}{2m_s}\frac{k_{jr}}{k_{jr}} + \delta_{ij}\frac{C_{jrs}}{C_{jr}}\frac{C_{jr}}{k_{jr}}\right)\frac{k_{jr}}{2u}\right]$$

$$= \frac{1}{2u}\sum_{i,j\in c}\left[\left(A_{ijs} - \gamma\frac{k_{is}k_{jr}}{2m_s}\right)\delta_{rs} - C_{jrs}\delta_{ij}\right]$$

where γ is resolution parameter related to time factor; A_{ijs} is the edge between intraslice node i and j; C_{jrs} denotes interslice coupling connecting node j in slice r and slice s; $k_{js} = \sum A_{ijs}$ denotes degree of node j in slice s; $c_{js} = \sum C_{jrs}$ denotes coupling intensity between other slices and node j in slice s; $k_{js} = k_{js}^r + c_{js}$ denotes connecting intensity between nodes in multislice network. Use the above as target function for optimization to discover the optimal community partition thereunder.

Laplacian dynamics-based research methods on multislice have wider applications than those based on static network, and allow community partition and quantification of partition quality of network under multiple time dimensions, multiple resolution parameter values and with multiple types of edges.

4.4.4 Detection of evolving virtual community based on clique percolation algorithm

Another analysis for detection of evolving community has evolved from a detection method of evolving community proposed in Reference [27] based on clique percolation (CPM) algorithm. The original intention of this method is to solve the member misjudgment problem for sequence of evolving community due to intercommunity overlap in the above-mentioned direct comparison method. When considering maximum community similarity, this method combines networks at adjacent moments before disintegration instead of directly comparing network community at adjacent moments. The method in Reference [27] uses clique percolation algorithm, which is an important method for static network community detection available for analyzing community structure with overlap. CPM algorithm thinks that community comprises a series of mutually-reachable k-cliques (full subgraph with scale of k). It combines adjacent k-cliques to detect communities and nodes within multiple communities are the overlap elements between communities. Dynamic nature of the network over time is revealed by discovering the relation between self-correlation function $C_A(t) = \frac{|A(t_0) \cap A(t_0+t)|}{|A(t_0) \cup A(t_0+t)|}$ and evolution of virtual community over time, with relatively obvious network change in relatively large scale. This overlap degree can be calculated through community structures at different moments in a composite graph by CPM in Figure 4.17.

Figure 4.17: Graph of calculating method for overlap degree in community evolution process (see Reference [27]).

As CPM algorithm can identify existing overlapping communities, the above evolved community detection method avoids misjudgment in such situations and can identify the members of evolved community sequence more accurately. However, this method has a defect, i.e. communities in network can be detected only by CPM algorithm during its implementation. Therefore, cross validation should be done on the results of evolved community sequence by other community partition technologies to improve the reliability of results.

4.4.5 Detection of evolving virtual community based on trend analysis on node behavior

Detection algorithm for evolving virtual community based on trend analysis on node behavior attribute dynamic evolution of virtual communities to node behavior, and analyze the effects of node behavior on network to determine possible evolution of virtual communities. As shown in Reference [24], enlarged virtual community with dynamic changes of members has longer life period; in contrast, small-scale virtual community with relatively stable community members has longer life period. Finally, community life period is predicted by analyzing the relation between internal and external members in the virtual community formed in network.

In Reference [24], connected edges between nodes in community can be classi-fied into two types: edges between such node and external nodes (intercommunity edge) and edges between such node and internal nodes (intracommunity edge). To inspect the relations between these variables, Reference [24] gives a quantified function $W_{out}/(W_{in}+W_{out})$, to denote the proportion of edges between internal node and external node and edges between internal nodes, where W_{out} is the weight sum of all intercommunity edges of all member nodes in community and W_{in} is the weight sum of all intracommunity edges of all member nodes in community, When such a proportion increases to a certain degree, it is possible for this node to leave current community and cause dynamic changes. When all nodes tend to leave current community, it may well disintegrate and vanish, i.e., correlation between community and its internal members and external members or communities can indicate community evolution trend.

In general, the above researches do not focus on prediction of evolving virtual community but on analysis of node evolution behavior. However, dynamic change of network and virtual communities is essentially caused by node evolution behavior, e.g. network (virtual community) structure change caused by node's exit from network (virtual community). Therefore, possible changes of virtual community structures can be predicted by behavior characteristics related to virtual communities. It is predictable that the thought of confirming possible evolved structure in network by analyzing node behavior trend will facilitate the promotion of new detection method for evolving virtual community.

4.5 Summary

In recent years, online social networking sites, microblogging, and other interactive internet services framed over the internet have gradually become the mainstream of information network application, and influential sits both at home and abroad, such as Facebook, Twitter, Sina Weibo, and renren.com, have become important platforms for social activities. Virtual community structure is an important structural characteristic of online social networks. Evolution of the virtual community of social network is closely associated with the network's functions, considerably affecting the propagation mode and law of information in social networks, as well as reflecting the characteristics and laws of human activity on social networks. Therefore, the evolution of the virtual communities has important research value and application prospects. This section introduces the research results of the evolution of virtual communities considering three aspects: the formation and emerging mechanisms of virtual communities, influencing factors on the evolution of virtual communities, and the detection algorithm of the evolution of virtual communities.

Research on static virtual community has developed over a decade generating relatively mature research results. However, research on the dynamically-evolved virtual communities in network is still in its initial stages. With the improvement of data acquisition and analysis technologies, the evolution and analysis problems of virtual communities will draw increasing attention from researchers. We believe that future research emphasis will be mainly on the following aspects:

1. With respect to detection algorithm for evolving virtual community, a key problem is how to construct reference graph with general applicability. At present, there are various types of reference graphs for static network but few for dynamically-evolving virtual community in network, and the existing reference graph has very narrow application scope. Therefore, it is an important problem to perfect existing theoretical model and thereby discover and construct effective dynamic reference graph.

2. Current researches focus on proposing different detection algorithm for evolving virtual community. It is still a problem to select a more effective detection method for evolving virtual community according to different types of networks. For this purpose, researchers are required to perform a comprehensive analysis on complexity, effectivity, comparison, and selection, etc., which is an important future research direction.

3. Is it possible to explore the internal mechanism of merging and evolution by tracing and analyzing evolution behavior of important virtual communities in network based on identifying and obtaining evolving virtual community sequence in dynamically-evolved network? This is also an important direction of merging and evolution mechanism research on virtual community in the future.

4. At present, there are rich research results for effect of network structure on information propagation but few for effect of information propagation on evolution of virtual community structure. Because virtual community constitutes an important part of network structure, it is an important and valuable problem to inspect the effect of information propagation in social networks on the evolution of virtual community structure. With the coming of big data era, these researches will also develop rapidly.

References

[1] Colizza V, Barrat A, Barthelemy M, Vespignani A: The role of the airline transportation network in the prediction and predictability of global epidemics. *Proc Natl Acad Sci* 2006, 103: 2015–2020.

[2] Bernardo MP, Garofalo F: Synchronizability and synchronization dynamics of weighed and unweighted scale free networks with degree mixing, 2007.

[3] Onnela JP, Saramäki J, Kertesz J, Kaski K: Intensity and coherence of motifs in weighted complex networks. *Phys Rev E* 2005, 71:065103.

[4] Granovetter M: The strength of weak ties. *Am J Sociol* 1973, 78:1360.

[5] Kossinets G, Watts JD: Empirical analysis of an evolving social network. *Science* 2006, 311:88–90.

[6] Kumpula J, Onnela JP, Saramaki J, Kaski K, Kartesz J: Emergence of communities in weighted networks. *Phys Rev Lett* 2007, 99:228701.
[7] Holme P, Kim BJ: Growing scale-free networks with tunable clustering. *Phys Rev E* 2002, 65:026107.
[8] Davidsen J, Ebel H, Bornholdt S: Emergence of a small world from local interactions: Modeling acquaintance networks. *Phys Rev Lett* 2002, 88:128701.
[9] Newman M, Strogatz SH, Watts DJ: Random graphs with arbitrary degree distributions and their applications. *Phys Rev E* 2001, 64:026118.
[10] Kleinberg J, Lawrence S: The structure of the web. *Science* 2001, 294:1849.
[11] Menczer F: Evolution of document networks. *Proc Natl Acad Sci* 2004, 101:5261–5265.
[12] Fenner T, Levene M, Loizou G, Wheeldon R: A stochastic model for the evolution of the web allowing link deletion. *ACM Transact Internet Tech* 2006, 6:117–130.
[13] Cheng XQ, Ren FX, Zhou S, Hu MB: Triangular clustering in document networks. *New J Phys* 2009, 11:033019.
[14] Ren FX, Shen HW, Cheng XQ: Modeling the clustering in citation networks. *Physica A* 2012, 391:3533–3539.
[15] Backstrom L, Huttenlocher D, Kleinberg J, Lan X: Group formation in large social networks: membership, growth, and evolution. In Proceedings of the 12th ACM SIGKDD International Conference on Knowledge Discovery and Data Mining. ACM, 2006.
[16] James Coleman. Foundations of Social Theory. Harvard,1990.
[17] Granovetter M: The strength of weak ties: A network theory revisited. *Sociol Theory* 1983, 1:201–233.
[18] Ugander J, Backstrom L, Marlow C, Kleinberg J: Structural diversity in social contagion. *Proc Natl Acad Sci* 2012, 109:5962–5966.
[19] Leskovec J, Huttenlocher D, Kleinberg J: Predicting positive and negative links in online social networks. In Proceedings of the 19th international conference on World Wide Web. ACM, 2010.
[20] Daniel Gruhl, Ramanathan Guha, et al. Information diffusion through blogspace. Proceedings of the 13th international conference on World Wide Web. ACM, 2004.
[21] Fritz H. Attitudes and cognitive organization. *J Psychol* 1946, 21:107–112.
[22] Cartwright D, Harary F: Structure balance: A generalization of Heider's theory. *Psychol Rev* 1956, 63:277–293.
[23] Yang B, You X, et al. Progress on analysis for detecting evolutionary community structure in complex dynamical networks. *Appl Res Comput* 2013, 30:1292–1296.
[24] Hopcroft J, Khan O, Kulis B, Selman B: Tracking evolving communities in large linked networks. *Proc Natl Acad Sci* 2004, 101:5249–5253.
[25] Greene D, Doyle D, Cunnigham P: Tracking the evolution of communities in dynamic social networks. In Proceedings of the 2nd International Conference on Advances in Social Networks Analysis and Mining. IEEE Computer Society, 2010 176–183.
[26] Takaffoli M, Sangi F, Fagnan J, Zaiane OR: Community evolution mining in dynamic social networks. *Proc Soc Behav Sci* 2011, 22:49–58.
[27] Palla G, Barabási AL, Vicsek T: Quantifying social group evolution. *Nature* 2007, 446:664–667.
[28] Chakrabarti D, Kumar R, Tomkins A: Evolutionary clustering. In Proceedings of the 12th ACM SIGKDD International Conference on Knowledge Discovery and Data Mining, 2006.
[29] Chi Y, Song X, Zhou D, Hino K, Tseng BL: Evolutionary spectral clustering by incorporating temporal smoothness. In Proceedings of the 13th ACM SIGKDD International Conference on Knowledge Discovery and Data Mining, 2007.
[30] Tang L, Liu H, Zhang J: Identifying involving groups in dynamic multimode networks. *IEEE T Knowl Data* En 2012, 24:72–85.

[31] Lin YR, Chi Y, Zhu S, Sundaram H, Tseng BL: FacetNet: A framework for analyzing communities and their evolutions in dynamic networks. In Proceedings of the 17th International Conference on World Wide Web, ACM, 2008.

[32] Selee TM, Kolda TG, Kegelmeyer WP, Griffin JD: Extracting clusters from large datasets with multiple similarity measures using IMSCAND. CSRI Summer Proceedings, 2007, 87–103.

[33] Lambiotte R, Delvenne JC, Barahona M: Laplacian dynamics and multiscale modular structure in networks. arXiv preprint arXiv: 0812.1770.

[34] Mucha PJ, Richardson T, Macon K, Porter MA, Onnela JP: Community structure in time-dependent, multiscale, and multiplex networks. *Science* 2010, 328:876–878.

Index

https://doi.org/10.1515/9783110599411-005

www.ingramcontent.com/pod-product-compliance
Lightning Source LLC
Chambersburg PA
CBHW060141060326
40690CB00018B/3940